"This series is a tremendous resource for those wanting to study and teach the Bible with an understanding of how the gospel is woven throughout Scripture. Here are gospel-minded pastors and scholars doing gospel business from all the Scriptures. This is a biblical and theological feast preparing God's people to apply the entire Bible to all of life with heart and mind wholly committed to Christ's priorities."

BRYAN CHAPELL, Chancellor, Covenant Theological Seminary

"Mark Twain may have smiled when he wrote to a friend, 'I didn't have time to write you a short letter, so I wrote you a long letter.' But the truth of Twain's remark remains serious and universal, because well-reasoned, compact writing requires extra time and extra hard work. And this is what we have in the Crossway Bible study series *Knowing the Bible*. The skilled authors and notable editors provide the contours of each book of the Bible as well as the grand theological themes that bind them together as one Book. Here, in a 12-week format, are carefully wrought studies that will ignite the mind and the heart."

R. KENT HUGHES, Senior Pastor Emeritus, College Church, Wheaton, Illinois

"*Knowing the Bible* brings together a gifted team of Bible teachers to produce a high-quality series of study guides. The coordinated focus of these materials is unique: biblical content, provocative questions, systematic theology, practical application, and the gospel story of God's grace presented all the way through Scripture."

PHILIP G. RYKEN, President, Wheaton College

"These *Knowing the Bible* volumes provide a significant and very welcome variation on the general run of inductive Bible studies. This series provides substantial instruction, as well as teaching through the very questions that are asked. *Knowing the Bible* then goes even further by showing how any given text links with the gospel, the whole Bible, and the formation of theology. I heartily endorse this orientation of individual books to the whole Bible and the gospel, and I applaud the demonstration that sound theology was not something invented later by Christians, but is right there in the pages of Scripture."

GRAEME L. GOLDSWORTHY, former lecturer, Moore Theological College; author, *According to Plan, Gospel and Kingdom, The Gospel in Revelation,* and *Gospel and Wisdom*

"What a gift to earnest, Bible-loving, Bible-searching believers! The organization and structure of the Bible study format presented through the *Knowing the Bible* series is so well conceived. Students of the Word are led to understand the content of passages through perceptive, guided questions, and they are given rich insights and application all along the way in the brief but illuminating sections that conclude each study. What potential growth in depth and breadth of understanding these studies offer! One can only pray that vast numbers of believers will discover more of God and the beauty of his Word through these rich studies."

BRUCE A. WARE, Professor of Christian Theology, The Southern Baptist Theological Seminary

D1531691

KNOWING THE BIBLE

J. I. Packer, Theological Editor
Dane C. Ortlund, Series Editor
Lane T. Dennis, Executive Editor

•   •   •   •   •   •

Genesis	Psalms	Jonah, Micah, and Nahum	Ephesians
Exodus	Proverbs	Haggai, Zechariah, and Malachi	Philippians
Leviticus	Ecclesiastes		Colossians and Philemon
Numbers	Song of Solomon	Matthew	
Deuteronomy	Isaiah	Mark	1–2 Thessalonians
Joshua	Jeremiah	Luke	1–2 Timothy and Titus
Judges	Lamentations, Habakkuk, and Zephaniah	John	
Ruth and Esther		Acts	Hebrews
1–2 Samuel	Ezekiel	Romans	James
1–2 Kings	Daniel	1 Corinthians	1–2 Peter and Jude
1–2 Chronicles	Hosea	2 Corinthians	1–3 John
Ezra and Nehemiah	Joel, Amos, and Obadiah	Galatians	Revelation
Job			

•   •   •   •   •   •

J. I. PACKER is Board of Governors' Professor of Theology at Regent College (Vancouver, BC). Dr. Packer earned his DPhil at the University of Oxford. He is known and loved worldwide as the author of the best-selling book *Knowing God*, as well as many other titles on theology and the Christian life. He serves as the General Editor of the ESV Bible and as the Theological Editor for the ESV *Study Bible*.

LANE T. DENNIS is President of Crossway, a not-for-profit publishing ministry. Dr. Dennis earned his PhD from Northwestern University. He is Chair of the ESV Bible Translation Oversight Committee and Executive Editor of the ESV *Study Bible*.

DANE C. ORTLUND is Executive Vice President of Bible Publishing and Bible Publisher at Crossway. He is a graduate of Covenant Theological Seminary (MDiv, ThM) and Wheaton College (BA, PhD). Dr. Ortlund has authored several books and scholarly articles in the areas of Bible, theology, and Christian living.

LUKE

A 12-WEEK STUDY

C. D. "Jimmy" Agan III

WHEATON, ILLINOIS

Crossway is a publishing ministry of Good News Publishers.

VP		29	28	27	26	25	24	23	22	21	20	19
14	13	12	11	10	9	8	7	6	5	4	3	2

TABLE OF CONTENTS

SERIES PREFACE

KNOWING THE BIBLE, as the series title indicates, was created to help readers know and understand the meaning, the message, and the God of the Bible. Each volume in the series consists of 12 units that progressively take the reader through a clear, concise study of that book of the Bible. In this way, any given volume can fruitfully be used in a 12-week format either in group study, such as in a church-based context, or in individual study. Of course, these 12 studies could be completed in fewer or more than 12 weeks, as convenient, depending on the context in which they are used.

Each study unit gives an overview of the text at hand before digging into it with a series of questions for reflection or discussion. The unit then concludes by highlighting the gospel of grace in each passage ("Gospel Glimpses"), identifying whole-Bible themes that occur in the passage ("Whole-Bible Connections"), and pinpointing Christian doctrines that are affirmed in the passage ("Theological Soundings").

The final component to each unit is a section for reflecting on personal and practical implications from the passage at hand. The layout provides space for recording responses to the questions proposed, and we think readers need to do this to get the full benefit of the exercise. The series also includes definitions of key words. These definitions are indicated by a note number in the text and are found at the end of each chapter.

Lastly, for help in understanding the Bible in this deeper way, we would urge the reader to use the ESV Bible and the *ESV Study Bible*, which are available online at esv.org. The *Knowing the Bible* series is also available online.

May the Lord greatly bless your study as you seek to know him through knowing his Word.

J. I. Packer
Lane T. Dennis

WEEK 1: OVERVIEW

Getting Acquainted

Like other Gospels, Luke's Gospel recounts the life, death, and resurrection of Jesus, the Son of God, who fulfills all of his Father's saving promises. Unlike other Gospels, Luke has a companion volume—Acts—in which salvation[1] advances, in Jesus' name, to "the end of the earth" (Acts 1:8). Luke's Gospel invites us to be part of this worldwide spread of the Christian message by showing how Jesus brings salvation to the last, the lost, and the least.

Luke's Gospel describes a world turned upside down. Sinners are saved while religious leaders are exposed as frauds. "Outsiders" embrace Jesus while "insiders" reject him. The poor rejoice while the rich are "sent away empty" (Luke 1:53). Because such paradoxes can create doubt, Luke writes to assure us that Jesus represents the fulfillment of God's saving purposes.

The most glaring paradox Luke presents is that of Jesus himself. No person has ever lived more faithfully than Jesus, yet no person has ever endured more suffering. As it points us to Jesus' cross and resurrection, Luke's Gospel prepares us to follow Jesus through hardship and humiliation, strengthened by faith in the God who exalts the lowly. (For further background, see the *ESV Study Bible*, pages 1935–1938, or visit esv.org.)

Placing It in the Larger Story

Luke's Gospel begins, and Acts ends, with a pointed reminder that the coming of Jesus fulfills God's promises, expressed in the Old Testament, to redeem[2] the world through Israel. As Luke's genealogy of Jesus makes clear, everyone who is descended from Adam—all humanity—has departed from God. Only "repentance and forgiveness of sins" (Luke 24:47) can restore us to the fullness of life that God intends for his human creatures. God's purpose is to raise up a king in Israel who can remove sin, defeat death, and pour out the life-giving power of the Holy Spirit on all who embrace his rule. Jesus is this messianic King, the greater "son of David" who brings God's promises to completion, and through whom "all flesh shall see the salvation of God" (Luke 3:6, citing Isa. 52:10).

Key Verse

"For the Son of Man came to seek and to save the lost." (Luke 19:10)

Date and Historical Background

Luke was likely written in the early 60s, sometime after the events described in Acts 28 but before two major events that are not mentioned in Luke or Acts—Paul's martyrdom in AD 64/65, and the destruction of the temple in AD 70. This means that Luke wrote within decades of Jesus' ministry and death.

In Luke's day, the Christian message had spread throughout Palestine, Asia Minor, Greece, and Rome. The stability of the Roman empire enabled Paul and other Christian missionaries to travel extensively, preaching to Jews and Gentiles alike. Both groups had difficulty accepting the possibility that a crucified man could be the Savior of the world—Jews because crucifixion represented a divine curse, and Gentiles because crucifixion represented weakness and humiliation. Other questions were raised by the fact that many Gentile "outsiders" were embracing Jesus, while many Jewish "insiders" continued to reject him and his followers. Luke wrote, at least in part, to reassure readers that the message about Jesus is true, despite such paradoxes. Today, Luke's Gospel continues to offer assurance to anyone who wrestles with the challenges of trusting and following Jesus.

Outline

I. The Prologue (1:1–4)

II. The Infancy Narrative (1:5–2:52)

A. The birth of John the Baptist foretold (1:5–25)

B. The birth of Jesus foretold (1:26–38)

C. Mary visits Elizabeth (1:39–56)

D. The birth of John the Baptist (1:57–80)

E. The birth of Jesus Christ (2:1–52)

III. Preparation for the Ministry of Jesus (3:1–4:15)

A. John the Baptist prepares the way (3:1–20)

B. Jesus' baptism, genealogy, and temptation (3:21–4:15)

IV. The Ministry of Jesus in Galilee (4:16–9:50)

A. The beginning (4:16–5:16)

B. The beginning of controversy (5:17–6:11)

C. Jesus teaches the disciples (6:12–49)

D. Who is this Jesus? (7:1–50)

E. Jesus teaches in parables (8:1–21)

F. Jesus is Lord of nature, demons, disease, and death (8:22–56)

G. Jesus and the Twelve (9:1–50)

V. The Journey to Jerusalem (9:51–19:27)

A. The first mention of the journey to Jerusalem (9:51–13:21)

B. The second mention of the journey to Jerusalem (13:22–17:10)

C. The third mention of the journey to Jerusalem (17:11–19:27)

VI. The Ministry of Jesus in Jerusalem (19:28–21:38)

A. The Triumphal Entry (19:28–40)

B. Jesus weeps over Jerusalem (19:41–44)

C. Jesus cleanses the temple (19:45–48)

D. The authority of Jesus challenged (20:1–8)

E. The parable of the wicked tenants (20:9–18)

F. Paying taxes to Caesar (20:19–26)

G. Sadducees ask about the resurrection (20:27–40)

H. Whose son is the Christ? (20:41–44)

I. Beware of the scribes (20:45–47)

J. The widow's offering (21:1–4)

K. Jesus foretells the destruction of the temple and Jerusalem (21:5–24)

L. Jesus foretells the coming of the Son of Man (21:25–38)

VII. The Suffering and Death of Jesus (22:1–23:56)

A. The plot to kill Jesus, and the Passover meal (22:1–38)

B. The arrest and trial (22:39–23:56)

VIII. The Resurrection of Jesus (24:1–53)

A. The empty tomb (24:1–12)

B. Jesus' appearance on the road to Emmaus (24:13–35)

C. Jesus appears to his disciples (24:36–49)

D. The ascension of Jesus (24:50–53)

▶ As You Get Started . . .

What teachings of Jesus or events from his life do you associate with Luke's Gospel in particular (as opposed to the Gospels of Matthew, Mark, and John)? (Hint: some of Jesus' best-known parables are found only in Luke.) How have these shaped your understanding of salvation?

What is your current understanding of how Luke's Gospel contributes to Christian theology? Are you aware of any ways in which this book clarifies our understanding of God, Jesus, the Holy Spirit, sin, salvation, or any other doctrine?

What aspects of Luke's Gospel would you like to understand better? Are there any specific questions that you hope to have answered through this study?

▶ As You Finish This Unit . . .

Take a few minutes to ask God to bless you with increased understanding and a transformed heart and life as you begin this study of Luke.

Definitions

[1] **Salvation** – Deliverance from the eternal consequences of sin, in order that one may completely enjoy all of God's promised blessings. Jesus' death and resurrection purchased salvation for believers.

[2] **Redeem** – In the context of the Bible, to buy back someone who had become enslaved or something that had been lost to someone else. Through his death and resurrection, Jesus purchased redemption from slavery to sin and its consequences for all believers (Col. 1:13–14).

Week 2: Sing for Joy— The Savior Is Born!

Luke 1:1–2:52

The Place of the Passage

After a brief prologue (Luke 1:1–4), Luke recounts the births of John the Baptist and Jesus. This section forms a link back to the Old Testament, so that we see these two births as means of fulfilling God's promises to redeem Israel and, through her, "all peoples" (2:31). The section also foreshadows major themes that will occur again and again throughout Luke's Gospel as this "good news of great joy" (v. 10) unfolds. In particular, we learn that while the proper response to the coming of Jesus is exuberant praise for God, this newborn King will also incite painful opposition (v. 34)—so that the shadow of the cross hangs even over the manger.

The Big Picture

Luke 1–2 presents Jesus as the fulfillment of God's saving promises, whose birth prompts joyful response on the part of God's people.

▶ Reflection and Discussion

Read through the complete passage for this study, Luke 1–2. Then review the questions below and write your notes on them concerning this introductory section of Luke's Gospel. (For further background, see the *ESV Study Bible*, pages 1942–1952, or visit www.esvbible.org.)

1. Luke's Prologue (1:1–4)

Theophilus (Luke 1:3) is likely a Gentile convert to Christianity. The themes of Luke and Acts suggest that such converts were experiencing a crisis of faith.[1] How does Luke's prologue offer reassurance to those whose beliefs are being challenged and undermined?

2. God Renews His Promises (1:5–38)

The story of Jesus, and of John as his forerunner, is a continuation of the story of the Old Testament. What features of Luke 1:5–38 as a whole make this clear, especially in light of Malachi 4:5–6?

How do Gabriel's words to Mary (Luke 1:30–37) indicate that God is doing something profoundly new in the birth of Jesus?

3. Songs of Salvation (1:39–80)

In this section, Mary and Zechariah offer poetic songs of praise to God. What do the opening verses of their songs teach us concerning the proper response to the good news about Jesus? What Old Testament promises do these songs present as fulfilled in Jesus?

Salvation is a key concept in Luke—and a complex one. What aspect of salvation is emphasized in Luke 1:77? In verses 74–75?

4. The Savior Is Born (2:1–20)

What does Jesus' birth in the city of Bethlehem tell us about his right to rule over Israel as God's chosen King (see Luke 1:32–33; 2:4, 11)? What does it suggest about the relationship between human power and divine providence[2] (see 2:1–4)?

13

In his message to the shepherds, an angel ascribes to Jesus three titles: Savior, Christ,[3] and Lord[4] (Luke 2:11). Taken separately, what does each title emphasize? Taken together, what paradoxical truth do these titles reveal about the baby Jesus?

5. Jesus in His Father's House (2:21–52)

In these verses, the tension between Jesus' true humanity and his divinity is especially clear. What features of the text suggest that Jesus is an ordinary child? What features indicate that he is the unique Son of God?

According to Luke 2:10, Jesus' birth represents great joy for "all the people." In the first century, this phrase would normally have been taken as a reference to the nation of Israel. How does Simeon's declaration in verses 29–32 expand our understanding?

Read through the following three sections on *Gospel Glimpses, Whole-Bible Connections,* and *Theological Soundings.* Then take time to consider the *Personal Implications* these sections may have for you.

Gospel Glimpses

THE GOD WHO EXALTS THE LOWLY. From the opening chapters of Luke's Gospel, we see that God works through the humble, weak, and needy. A child-less, aged couple; a young virgin in her "humble estate" (Luke 1:48); lowly shepherds; an elderly widow—all have their place in the fulfillment of God's world-changing purposes. Since the coming of Jesus demonstrates God's choice to save the world through weakness, we are left with no choice but to celebrate God's power (vv. 46–55). The climactic demonstration of this pattern is Jesus' death and resurrection. At the cross God saves the world through weakness, and in the resurrection God exercises his power on behalf of the One who humbled himself "to the point of death" (Phil. 2:8–11). From start to finish, the gospel calls us to humble ourselves, trusting in God's strength rather than our own.

THE RHYTHM OF SALVATION. In Luke 1–2, we hear a threefold rhythm—of need, deliverance, and response—that characterizes all of God's gracious deal-ings with sinners. First, we detect our deep need for salvation. So profound is this need that the Son of God himself must put on flesh and blood and enter our world as "Savior" (2:11) to rescue us from sin and all its consequences. Second, we see God's initiative to provide for us what we cannot provide for ourselves. God sends Jesus as our Savior, not in response to any human action but in fulfillment of his own promises. Finally, we note that God's provision of a Savior prompts joy, praise, and thanksgiving on the part of his people.

Whole-Bible Connections

GOD'S TEMPLE AS A GATEWAY TO THE WORLD. The opening scenes of Luke's Gospel revolve around the temple in Jerusalem, where we learn that Jesus will be the Savior of Israel (Luke 1:16; 2:25, 38) and of "all peoples" (2:31; see also v. 32). From Old Testament times, God intended the temple to be a light to the nations, a place where worship and sacrifice would point all human beings to the one true God (Psalms 96; 98; 102; Isa. 60:1–7; 62:1–12; 66:18–23; Jer. 3:17). Jesus, zealous for his Father's house (John 2:17; Ps. 69:9), not only goes there as a boy to learn the Scriptures, but also returns in adulthood to oppose those who have forgotten that the temple is to be "a house of prayer for all peoples" (Isa. 56:7; compare Mark 11:17; Luke 19:46). Through the outpouring of the Holy Spirit, Jesus makes the church his new temple (1 Cor. 3:16–17; 2 Cor. 6:16; Eph. 2:19–22), the dwelling place through which the world encounters the living God.

GOD'S ANOINTED KING. At creation, God appointed his image-bearers to rule over creation (Gen. 1:26–28; Ps. 8:6–8). Because of our sin, human beings are now under the rule of sin, death, and decay (Rom. 8:20–21). Since our fall into sin, therefore, God's purpose has been to raise up a king who could faithfully bear the divine image, deliver us from our enemies, and reign over us so that we can share in all the benefits of his kingdom rule. God promised David that one of his descendants would be such a king (2 Sam. 7:8–17; Ps. 89:3–4). Jesus is the greater Son of David (Luke 1:32, 69; 18:38) who is now enthroned at God's right hand (Acts 2:33; 5:31), and who will one day return to destroy our final enemy, death (1 Cor. 15:20–26), so that we may share resurrection life with him forever.

▶ Theological Soundings

DIVINE REVELATION. Luke sees his Gospel as a continuation of the Old Testament, and therefore as a reliable record of God's saving deeds. God reveals himself in ways that human beings can clearly understand, whether through visions (Luke 1:22), angelic messengers, or the promises, prophecies, and instructions of the Old Testament. God makes himself known most clearly through the person, words, and work of Jesus, who is "a light for revelation" (2:32) to Jew and Gentile alike.

THE VIRGIN BIRTH OF THE SON OF GOD. Luke wants us to see immediately that Jesus is a real human being, born of a woman, with a body and personality that undergo development (Luke 2:52). But Luke also wants us to see much more than this. John may be the "prophet of the Most High" (1:76), but Jesus is the "Son of the Most High" (1:32). John's birth to a childless couple is shocking, but Jesus' birth from a virgin as a result of the Holy Spirit's power (v. 35) is a miracle unparalleled in Scripture. Our Savior's supernatural birth forms the foundation for all of Christian belief concerning him.

▶ Personal Implications

Take time to reflect on the implications of Luke 1–2 for your own life today. Consider what you have learned that might lead you to praise God, repent of sin, and trust more deeply in his gracious promises. Make notes below on the personal implications for your walk with the Lord of the (1) *Gospel Glimpses*, (2) *Whole-Bible Connections*, (3) *Theological Soundings*, and (4) this passage as a whole.

1. Gospel Glimpses

2. Whole-Bible Connections

3. Theological Soundings

4. Luke 1–2

> ## As You Finish This Unit . . .

Take a moment now to ask for the Lord's blessing and help as you continue in this study of Luke. And take a moment also to look back through this unit of study, to reflect on some key things that the Lord may be teaching you—and perhaps to highlight and underline these things to review again in the future.

Definitions

[1] **Faith** – Trust in or reliance upon something or someone outside ourselves. Salvation, which is purely a work of God's grace, can be received only through faith (Rom. 5:2; Eph. 2:8–9). The writer of Hebrews calls on believers to emulate those who lived godly lives by faith (Hebrews 11). Faith in Jesus involves both trusting his teaching and trusting him as living Savior and Lord (John 5:46–47; 20:27–29).

[2] **Providence** – God's good, wise, and sovereign guidance and control of all things, by which he supplies all our needs and accomplishes his holy will.

[3] **Christ** – Transliteration of the Greek for "anointed one" (equivalent to Hebrew *Messiah*). The term is used throughout the NT as a title for Jesus, indicating his role as Messiah and Savior.

[4] **Lord** – Someone superior in authority or status to another, similar to "master." It is a common translation for several different Hebrew titles for God in the OT, and in the NT regularly refers to Jesus. Greek speakers used the term to translate the Hebrew *Yahweh* (*YHWH*), the personal name of God.

WEEK 3: OUR REDEEMER IS READY

Luke 3:1–4:15

▲

The Place of the Passage

Following the births of John the Baptist and Jesus, Luke focuses on three events that prepare for Jesus' public ministry. First, John's ministry prepares the people to receive Jesus' work as Messiah.[1] Second, Jesus' baptism shows him to be empowered by the Holy Spirit to serve the purposes of the Father who loves him. Third, Jesus' wilderness temptation demonstrates his readiness to defeat sin and Satan as our victorious, sinless Savior. Luke includes a genealogy that draws attention to Jesus as a "second Adam" who reverses the consequences of Adam's failure. The section assures us that Jesus' work as Messiah—including his death, which is foreshadowed in important ways—is acceptable to God, and therefore able to redeem sinners.

The Big Picture

Luke 3:1–4:15 deepens our trust in Jesus by assuring us that he is fully and uniquely prepared to serve as our Savior.

Reflection and Discussion

Read through the complete passage for this study, Luke 3:1–4:15. Then review the questions below and write your notes on them concerning this section of Luke's Gospel. (For further background, see the *ESV Study Bible*, pages 1952–1955, or visit www.esvbible.org.)

1. The Ministry of John the Baptist (3:1–20)

What hints does this section provide that Jesus' ministry will benefit a wide range of people, and not just those who are ethnically Jewish or outwardly religious?

What "fruits" does John the Baptist cite as evidence of genuine repentance[2] before God? What does this suggest about the kind of kingdom Jesus has come to establish?

Readers of Luke 1–2 already know that Jesus is no ordinary human. What details of this section confirm that conclusion?

2. The Baptism and Genealogy of the Son of God (3:21–38)

What features of Luke 3:16–22 suggest that Jesus' baptism is unique, and not (as in the case of other people; see 3:3) an expression of personal repentance? If not to confess his own sin, why does Jesus submit to John's baptism?

How did Adam, whom Luke calls "the son of God" (Luke 3:38), prove to be a faithless son, and what were the results of his failure? What does this imply about the ministry of Jesus, who is both the "second Adam," and the greater Son of God?

3. The Temptation of the Son of God (4:1–15)

Take a moment to summarize the similarities and differences between Jesus' temptation and Adam's fall into sin (Gen. 3:1–6). Note especially the circumstances in which each is tested and the settings in which their tests occur. How does this deepen your appreciation for Jesus and his faithfulness?

Three times Jesus responds to Satan with Scripture citations from the book of Deuteronomy. How do Deuteronomy 8:1–18 and 6:10–19 suggest that Satan is tempting Jesus not simply to a one-time sin but to a mindset of self-reliance? How do these texts highlight the contrast between Israel's failures and Jesus' faithfulness?

In Luke's day, it was commonly assumed that true greatness was incompatible with suffering, deprivation, and humiliation. How does Satan apply similar logic as he tempts Jesus? What details of Luke 4:9–13 foreshadow the fact that Jesus will endure ultimate suffering on the cross?

Read through the following three sections on *Gospel Glimpses*, *Whole-Bible Connections*, and *Theological Soundings*. Then take time to consider the *Personal Implications* these sections may have for you.

▶ Gospel Glimpses

GOOD NEWS THROUGH BAD NEWS. The biblical gospel of salvation involves a paradox. On the one hand, salvation implies deliverance from impending disaster; on the other, it implies that without this deliverance, disaster will overwhelm us—as John's preaching makes clear (Luke 3:9, 17). But when the Holy Spirit brings us to repentance, we freely confess our desperate wickedness, our liability to God's judgment, and our inability to deliver ourselves. In turn, John's message of "good news" (v. 18) becomes even more wonderful: on all who turn to him as Savior, Jesus will pour out not judgment but the life-giving Spirit of God!

THE HUMBLE SAVIOR. Jesus is "the Lord" (Luke 3:4), one whose feet John is unworthy to touch (v. 16). But in the logic of the gospel, such greatness goes hand in hand with deep humility. Thus Jesus, the "mightier" one (v. 16), submits to John's baptism, expressing his solidarity with sinners. Some even mistake him for a mere son of Joseph (v. 23). According to Satan, Jesus should be immune to suffering if he is the Son of God; yet this status only strengthens Jesus' resolve to endure affliction. And so we see, even before his public ministry begins, that Jesus is a humble Servant-King whose greatness will be most powerfully displayed in weakness.

Whole-Bible Connections

JESUS, ADAM, AND ISRAEL. When Luke calls Adam "the son of God" (Luke 3:38), he is reminding us that in the beginning, God gave life to Adam, calling him to bear God's image faithfully, caring (with Eve) for the earth in a way that would cause life to flourish under God's design (Gen. 1:26–28). Instead, Adam rebelled, bringing sin, death, and the curse to God's good world (Genesis 3). In response, God raised up another "son," the people of Israel (Ex. 4:22; Hos. 11:1; Rom. 9:4), whose mission was to bear witness among the nations to the one true and living God. Instead, Israel turned repeatedly to idols, hindering rather than promoting God's redeeming purposes. Jesus' mission as the Son of God reverses the failure of these faithless sons, so that as adopted sons and daughters (Rom. 8:15–17; Gal. 4:4–7; 1 John 3:1) we too can advance our Father's life-giving mission.

GOD THE JUDGE. The whole Bible reflects the truth that God, "the Judge of all the earth" (Gen. 18:25), has the right to evaluate the hearts and deeds of all his creatures. God's judgment can bring terror to those under his wrath (Ps. 94:2; Isa. 11:4; Ezek. 7:3) or joy to those who await the verdict that will put all things right (1 Chron. 16:33; Ps. 67:4; 96:10–13; Lam. 3:59). Jesus, who came to endure God's judgment and wrath on our behalf at the cross (2 Cor. 5:21; Gal. 3:13), will one day return to carry out the final judgment (Matt. 25:31–46; Acts 10:42; 2 Tim. 4:1). Because Jesus' work enables God to enforce his justice while saving sinners, we can cry, "Hallelujah! Salvation and glory and power belong to our God, for his judgments are true and just" (Rev. 19:1–2).

Theological Soundings

THE HISTORICAL RELIABILITY OF SCRIPTURE. Luke cites concrete facts that are open to historical investigation (Luke 3:1–2, 19, 23–38), indicating his own confidence in the truthfulness of the events he reports. Even where difficulties arise, as when we compare the genealogy of Jesus found in Matthew 1:1–17 with that found in Luke 3:23–38, apparent contradictions can be reconciled (see the discussion of this passage in the *ESV Study Bible*, page 1954). Many tensions are resolved when we give careful attention to the details of the biblical text, especially regarding issues of chronology (compare "Then," which begins Matt. 4:5, with the less chronologically strict "And" which begins Luke 4:9).

THE DOCTRINE OF THE TRINITY.[3] In this section Luke portrays each member of the Trinity as being a distinct person capable of acting purposefully: the Spirit fills and leads the Son (Luke 3:22; 4:1, 14); Jesus the Son prays, resists temptation, and teaches (3:21; 4:2–15); the Father loves and receives worship from the Son (3:22; 4:8). Yet Luke describes these three in ways that highlight the unity they share; for example, the Spirit empowers the Son to remain faithful to the Father's purposes (4:1, 14). Though Luke offers no explanation of the doctrine of the Trinity, his Gospel assumes a complete unity among three divine persons—a unity without which our salvation could not have been accomplished.

JESUS' SINLESSNESS. Several features of Luke 3:1–4:15 indicate that Jesus is sinless: (1) Jesus must possess a supernatural degree of holiness in order to baptize others with the Holy Spirit (3:16); (2) Jesus is able to judge others for their sins (3:17); (3) God is "well pleased" with his Son (3:22), words not spoken about any others who received John's baptism; (4) the second Adam (3:38) can redeem us from Adam's failure only if he does not share in Adam's sin; and (5) even when directly confronted by Satan, Jesus faithfully resists temptation. Luke's portrayal of Jesus is consistent with other biblical writers who state explicitly that Jesus was without sin (2 Cor. 5:21; Heb. 4:15; 1 Pet. 2:22; 1 John 3:5).

> ## Personal Implications

Take time to reflect on the implications of Luke 3:1–4:15 for your own life today. Consider what you have learned that might lead you to praise God, repent of sin, and trust more deeply in his gracious promises. Make notes below on the personal implications for your walk with the Lord of the (1) *Gospel Glimpses*, (2) *Whole-Bible Connections*, (3) *Theological Soundings*, and (4) this passage as a whole.

1. Gospel Glimpses

2. Whole-Bible Connections

3. Theological Soundings

4. Luke 3:1–4:15

> ## As You Finish This Unit . . .

Take a moment now to ask for the Lord's blessing and help as you continue in this study of Luke. And take a moment also to look back through this unit of study, to reflect on some key things that the Lord may be teaching you—and perhaps to highlight and underline these things to review again in the future.

Definitions

[1] **Messiah** – A transliteration of a Hebrew word meaning "anointed one," the equivalent of the Greek word *Christ*. Originally applied to anyone specially designated for a particular role, such as king or priest. Jesus himself affirmed that he was the Messiah sent from God (Matt. 16:16–17).

[2] **Repentance** – A complete change of heart and mind regarding one's overall attitude toward God and one's individual actions. True regeneration and conversion are always accompanied by repentance.

[3] **Trinity** – The Godhead as it exists in three distinct Persons: Father, Son, and Holy Spirit. There is one God, yet he is three Persons; there are not three Gods, nor do the three Persons merely represent different aspects or modes of a single God. While the term Trinity is not found in the Bible, the concept is repeatedly assumed and affirmed by the writers of Scripture (e.g., Matt. 28:19; Luke 1:35; 3:22; Gal. 4:6; 2 Thess. 2:13–14; Heb. 10:29).

WEEK 4: SALVATION COMES WITH POWER

Luke 4:16–6:49

The Place of the Passage

Luke's account of Jesus' public ministry opens with a sermon in the synagogue at Nazareth (Luke 4:16–30), introducing four themes that characterize Jesus' ministry as a whole: (1) Jesus' authority as Messiah to "proclaim liberty to the captives" and actually "to set [them] at liberty" (v. 18b); (2) Jesus' saving power to perform miracles; (3) Jesus' willingness to extend salvation to the unclean, the outcast, and even to Gentiles; and (4) the hostility Jesus encounters from those who resist his priorities. In the events that follow, Jesus heals various people, enters into disputes over his authority, and calls disciples who will help him multiply his ministry. The section ends with the "Sermon on the Plain," where Jesus summarizes the blessings and responsibilities that are ours as his disciples.

The Big Picture

Luke 4:16–6:49 shows us Jesus' authority to proclaim—and effect—salvation. It also shows us what it means to be a disciple who benefits from and participates in his saving work.

27

> ## Reflection and Discussion

Read through the complete passage for this study, Luke 4:16–6:49. Then review the questions below and write your notes on them concerning this section of Luke's Gospel. (For further background, see the *ESV Study Bible*, pages 1955–1964, or visit esv.org.)

1. Jesus' Sermon at Nazareth (4:16–30)

Several facts make Jesus' sermon startling: (1) Jesus does not cite the entirety of Isaiah 61:2, omitting a reference to coming judgment; (2) Jesus cites Isaiah 58:6 instead, claiming authority not only to *announce* but also to *accomplish* salvation; and (3) he refers to Elijah and Elisha (Luke 4:24–27), who ministered during a time of large-scale rebellion by Israel against God. How do these factors help to explain the angry response provoked by Jesus' message?

Is Jesus' sermon concerned with redeeming people from *physical* bondage or from *spiritual* bondage? Here and in the Beatitudes of Luke 6:20–23, is Jesus proclaiming good news to people who are materially poor, spiritually poor, or both?

2. Saving Power, Seeds of Conflict, and
Appointing Apostles (4:31–6:16)

In this section of Luke, how does Jesus demonstrate his power—over nature, over people, or over sin and its consequences? How do different characters or groups model appropriate response to such power?

How do Jesus' actions in this section confirm the message of his Nazareth sermon—namely, that he will use his authority as Messiah to extend salvation to the outcast and the needy?

According to Luke, some religious authorities fear that Jesus encourages (Luke 5:30), or even commits (v. 21), sin. What is Jesus' true impact on sinners, as revealed in his interaction with Peter (v. 8), the paralytic (vv. 20–24), and Levi (vv. 27–32)?

Religious leaders also demonstrate concern that Jesus disregards God's law. How does Jesus demonstrate respect for God's law in Luke 5:14? Given that one of the original purposes of Sabbath law was to bring rest to the weary

(Ex. 20:8–10; Deut. 5:12–15), how do Jesus' actions in Luke 6:1–11 represent a *fulfillment*, rather than a violation, of God's law?

How do Luke 6:13 and 6:17 indicate that Luke is using the word "disciple" to represent a larger group than the 12 apostles? If the Sermon on the Plain represents Jesus' kingdom-advancing instructions for every disciple, what is the special kingdom-multiplying mission for which he appoints apostles (see 4:43; 5:10; and the note on Mark 3:14–15 in the ESV *Study Bible*, page 1898)?

3. The Sermon on the Plain (6:17–49)

In order to make us fit to meet the demands of discipleship, Jesus must give us a new perspective on life in the kingdom of God.[1] After reading the beatitudes and woes of Luke 6:20–26, how would you summarize the major themes of this new perspective?

What are the duties of discipleship as presented in Luke 6:27–49? Put another way, what priorities should characterize the life of a "fully trained" (v. 40) disciple of Jesus?

According to Luke 6:43–45, who will be able to bear the good fruit of obedience to Jesus' teaching? What does this imply about the depth of sin's corrupting power, and our need for God's transforming grace?

Read through the following three sections on *Gospel Glimpses, Whole-Bible Connections*, and *Theological Soundings*. Then take time to consider the *Personal Implications* these sections may have for you.

Gospel Glimpses

THE MULTIPLE DIMENSIONS OF SAVING GRACE. The salvation that Jesus brings includes deliverance from God's judgment (Luke 6:24–26, 49) through the forgiveness of sin (5:24). But as this section of Luke's Gospel attests, salvation also entails deliverance from physical ailments, from Satanic spiritual powers, from the burdens of poverty, oppression, and persecution—and even from the fruitless toil that is a consequence of Adam's sin (5:5–6; compare Gen. 3:17–19). The good news of the gospel cannot be reduced to one dimension, because our Savior's grace extends to every aspect of human need.

POWER FOR THE POWERLESS. Jesus' ministry assumes human inability: the poor have no resources to improve their condition; the captives cannot liberate themselves; the blind cannot open their own eyes (Luke 4:18). At the level of the heart, the same is true, for a thornbush cannot transform itself into a fig tree (6:43–45). But Luke repeatedly reminds us (4:36; 5:17, 24; 6:19) that Jesus has power to heal both body and soul, doing for us what we cannot do for ourselves. God graciously provides for those who otherwise have no hope—a truth that characterizes every aspect of Jesus' saving work.

LOVE FOR ENEMIES. Jesus' call to do good to those who injure or insult us is inescapably clear, but where will sinners find the strength to repay curse with blessing? The answer lies in the love of our heavenly Father, who is "kind to the ungrateful and evil" (Luke 6:35). Strength to show mercy to others is found in God's mercy to us (v. 36). We see such mercy when Jesus answers those who persecute him not with "wrath" (4:28) or "fury" (6:11) but with words of patient warning (vv. 24–26).

Whole-Bible Connections

THE SABBATH. In Genesis, we learn that on the seventh day God "rested" to demonstrate satisfaction with his work of creating (Gen. 2:2–3; Heb. 4:4). After Adam's fall, the Sabbath becomes an expression of divine grace to those wearied by toil and anxiety; thus Israel's Sabbath rest expresses trust in God's provision (Ex. 20:8–11; Lev. 25:6–7, 12) and gratitude for deliverance from slavery (Deut. 5:12–15). Jesus rebukes religious leaders who distort the fourth commandment by focusing solely on its prohibition against work, since this ignores the positive call of the Sabbath to relieve others from wearisome burdens so that they might enjoy God's blessings (Isa. 56:1–8; 58:3–14; Matt. 12:7; John 5:8–17). Following Jesus' resurrection, we gather for worship on the first day of the week (Matt. 28:1; Acts 20:7; 1 Cor. 16:2), "the Lord's day" (Rev. 1:10). This pattern of weekly rest and renewal strengthens our longing for the eternal rest that we already enjoy in Christ (Matt. 11:28–30; Heb. 4:3, 9–10; Rev. 6:11; 14:13) and that all creation will enjoy fully at his return (Rom. 8:19–23).

Theological Soundings

THE REALITY OF MIRACLES.[2] Biblical faith has always affirmed God's supernatural power to perform deeds that are outside normal human expectations. While Luke's Gospel does not discuss the scientific and philosophical framework for understanding miracles, it clearly portrays Jesus' power to heal (Luke 4:23, 38–40; 5:12–15, 17–26; 6:6–10, 18–19), to cast out demons (4:31–36, 41; 6:18), and to control nature (5:1–9). Neither legends nor exaggerated accounts of natural phenomena, biblical miracles call us to embrace the lordship of Father, Son, and Spirit over all of creation.

UNIVERSAL DEPRAVITY.[3] Scripture teaches that because of Adam's sin, every human being is born in a state of rebellion against God from which we are helpless to deliver ourselves (Rom. 3:23; 5:12–21; 8:1–8). According to Jesus, our evil words and deeds reflect the evil in our hearts (Luke 6:43–45). Therefore, in order for us to dwell in God's presence, our sin must be forgiven (5:8); this is, in fact, our most pressing need (vv. 17–26). (Luke 5:32 may seem to indicate that some are not sinful, but here Jesus employs sarcasm to teach that his ministry will not benefit anyone who refuses to admit his or her need of forgiveness.) Thankfully, Jesus is a merciful physician who not only diagnoses our sinful state but also heals it (v. 31).

Personal Implications

Take time to reflect on the implications of Luke 4:16–6:49 for your own life today. Consider what you have learned that might lead you to praise God, repent of sin, and trust more deeply in his gracious promises. Make notes below on the personal implications for your walk with the Lord of the (1) *Gospel Glimpses*, (2) *Whole-Bible Connections*, (3) *Theological Soundings*, and (4) this passage as a whole.

1. Gospel Glimpses

2. Whole-Bible Connections

3. Theological Soundings

4. Luke 4:16–6:49

► As You Finish This Unit . . .

Take a moment now to ask for the Lord's blessing and help as you continue in this study of Luke. And take a moment also to look back through this unit of study, to reflect on some key things that the Lord may be teaching you—and perhaps to highlight and underline these things to review again in the future.

Definitions

[1] **Kingdom of God** – The sovereign, life-giving rule of God. At the present time, God's kingdom can be found in heaven and among his people (Matt. 6:9–10; Luke 17:20–21), even though this fallen, sinful world does not submit to God's rule. After Christ returns, however, the kingdom of the world will become the kingdom of God (Rev. 11:15). Then all people will, either willingly or regretfully, acknowledge his sovereignty (Phil. 2:9–11). Even the natural world will be transformed to operate in perfect harmony with God (Rom. 8:19–23).

[2] **Miracle** – A special act of God that goes beyond natural means, thus demonstrating his power.

[3] **Depravity** – The sinful condition of human nature apart from grace, whereby humans are inclined to serve their own will and to reject God's rule.

WEEK 5: GREATER THAN A PROPHET, MORE HUMBLE THAN A KING

Luke 7:1–9:50

The Place of the Passage

This portion of Luke's Gospel weaves together Jesus' words and deeds in a way that repeatedly challenges our expectations: Gentiles trust Jesus more than Israelites (Luke 7:9); sinners embrace the forgiveness Jesus offers while religious leaders reject him (7:29–35); and those who have no food eat their fill (9:12–17). But the most shocking reversal has to do with Jesus' identity as the Messiah (v. 20): John the Baptist expects a display of messianic might; Pharisees look for someone who keeps a safe distance from sinners; even Jesus' closest followers are unprepared to hear that Jesus, the Messiah, will die. As our expectations about Jesus are reshaped, so is our understanding of what it means to hear him, trust him, and follow him.

The Big Picture

Luke 7:1–9:50 portrays Jesus as more powerful and glorious than the greatest of prophets, but also as one who is doubted, rejected, and destined to die.

Reflection and Discussion

Read through the complete passage for this study, Luke 7:1–9:50. Then review the questions below and write your notes on them concerning this section of Luke's Gospel. (For further background, see the *ESV Study Bible*, pages 1964–1974, or visit esv.org.)

1. One Greater Than a Prophet (7:1–50)

How does Jesus' raising of the widow's son (Luke 7:11–17) show him to be a greater prophet than Elijah, who performed a similar miracle in 1 Kings 17:17–24? How does the centurion's faith in Jesus (Luke 7:2–10) illustrate the truth taught in 1 Kings 17:24?

What might have led John to be "offended" (Luke 7:23) by Jesus? How does Jesus' response demonstrate that he is in fact the Messiah, even if not the kind that John had expected?

Given Luke 3:3 as background, how does the failure of religious leaders to receive John's baptism represent a rejection of God's purpose (7:30)? According to 7:36–50, what actions or attitudes might indicate whether a person is rejecting or embracing God's purpose?

2. Ears to Hear (8:1–21)

According to Jesus, we should "take care then how [we] hear" the word of God (Luke 8:18). In these verses, what are some marks of careful hearing of the word? What are some marks of careless hearing?

What evidence do we have that the women of Luke 8:2–3 are hearing carefully?

3. Fear versus Faith (8:22–56)

Each of the miracles of Luke 8:22–56 highlights the distinction between fear and faith. Which characters in these accounts demonstrate fear, and what are they afraid of? In what ways are their fears appropriate or inappropriate?

What is it about Jesus that comforts the fears of others—that is, how does Jesus call forth faith from those who might otherwise be overcome by fear?

4. Sharing the Ministry—and Destiny— of a Cross-Bearing King (9:1–50)

In Luke 9:1, Jesus entrusts the 12 apostles with "power and authority" to extend his ministry. How do verses 3–9 indicate that these privileges will be accompanied by deprivation, rejection, and persecution? How should the miracle of verses 10–17 encourage the apostles amid such difficulties?

In Jesus' day, the term "Christ" (Luke 9:20) was associated with kingship, and therefore with glory and power. How do verses 26–35 and 42–43 confirm those associations? How do Jesus' predictions of his own fate (vv. 22, 44) alter this understanding?

Jesus says that he will endure great suffering and death before he enters his glory. What implications does this have for all who follow and serve Jesus (see Luke 9:23, 48)? What factors keep Jesus' followers from embracing those implications (see vv. 45–50)?

Read through the following three sections on *Gospel Glimpses*, *Whole-Bible Connections*, and *Theological Soundings*. Then take time to consider the *Personal Implications* these sections may have for you.

Gospel Glimpses

WELCOMING THE OUTCAST. In Luke 7:1–9:50, Jesus repeatedly ministers to people at the fringes of society. More than this, Jesus identifies himself with the outcast: he is "a friend of tax collectors and sinners" (7:34, 39) who calls a once-unclean woman his "daughter" (8:48) and equates receiving a child with "receiv[ing] me" (9:48). As he goes on to bear the shame of crucifixion,[1] Jesus makes himself an outcast so that we might be welcomed into his Father's family.

GRACE AS THE POWER FOR LOVE. Luke 7:36–50 reveals the power source for radical obedience: love prompted by redeeming grace. The forgiven woman demonstrates love for Jesus in ways that far exceed normal expressions of hospitality (vv. 44–47). The more we appreciate our desperate need for forgiveness, the more we will love the Savior who forgives—and the more power we will have to express this love for him in deeds of service and obedience.

THE GOOD NEWS OF CROSS BEARING. Jesus' command to deny ourselves and take up a cross (Luke 9:23) may not sound like good news. But this weighty demand is a source of great freedom: like criminals walking to the place of execution, we are free to focus on what matters most, undistracted by "the cares and riches and pleasures of life" (8:14). More important, Jesus has already announced that he will bear a cross of his own (9:21–22). Strength to die to ourselves comes from following the Savior who lays down his life for us.

Whole-Bible Connections

SEEING BUT NOT SEEING. In Isaiah 6:9–10, God warned the prophet that many would grasp the content of his message yet reject its truth. In Luke 8:10 (and parallels in Matt. 13:13–15; Mark 4:12; see also John 12:37–41; Acts 28:25–28), Jesus cites these verses to show that his parables have a similar function. They are simple stories full of everyday images, yet they require us to admit that we—like Isaiah's audience (see Isaiah 1–4)—are rebels in need of God's forgiveness. To genuinely embrace such truth requires insight that only God's Spirit can give (1 Cor. 2:12–14).

GOD'S PURPOSE. Luke speaks of "the purpose of God" (Luke 7:30; see also Acts 2:23; 4:28; 13:36; 20:27) to indicate that Jesus' work fulfills a plan of salvation that runs throughout Scripture. By restoring Jew and Gentile alike to himself (Luke 24:46–47; Rom. 4:1–17), God fulfills his promise to bless all nations through Abraham's descendants (Gen. 12:2–3; 26:4; Acts 3:25; Gal. 3:8). So that this blessedness may abound forever in all the earth, God sends Jesus to establish a never-ending kingdom of peace (Luke 1:33, 51–53, 68–75; Rom. 8:18–23;

2 Pet. 3:13; Rev. 21:3–4). When we embrace Jesus, we put ourselves at the heart of this glorious purpose.

JESUS' EXODUS. At the Mount of Transfiguration,[2] Moses and Elijah discuss with Jesus his approaching "departure" (Luke 9:31). Luke's Greek word, *exodos*, can refer to death (as in 2 Pet. 1:15) or to Israel's exodus from Egypt (as in Heb. 11:22). Luke's play on words reminds us that Jesus is greater than Moses and Elijah. His death and resurrection lead us not just from slavery and into the Promised Land, but from bondage to sin (Rom. 8:15, 21; Titus 3:3; Heb. 2:15) and into eternal fellowship with God in the new heaven and new earth (Isa. 65:17–25; Rev. 21:1–4).

Theological Soundings

SALVATION BY FAITH. According to Ephesians 2:8–9, we are saved "by grace . . . through faith. And this is . . . not a result of works, so that no one may boast." This doctrine is affirmed in Luke 7:1–10, where a group of Jewish elders commend a centurion as "worthy" based on his deeds, the centurion responds that he is "not worthy," and Jesus commends him for "such faith." True faith leads to good works but does not treat them as a means for securing Jesus' favor.

THE DEITY OF CHRIST. Numerous details from this section of Luke confirm the church's confession that Jesus is God incarnate. First, Jesus is able to raise the dead by his own authority (Luke 7:14–16; 8:54). Second, Jesus sovereignly commands the wind and waves (8:24–25). Third, there is no distinction between "how much God has done" for the Gerasene demoniac and "how much Jesus" has done for him (8:39). Finally, Jesus shares in his Father's glory (9:26, 29, 34). Though mystery surrounds the incarnation,[3] it is clear that Jesus is God in human flesh.

PERSEVERANCE OF THE SAINTS. Jesus' parable of the sower sheds light on the difficult question of whether a true disciple of Christ can finally fall away from the faith. Some may initially appear to have saving faith in Jesus, but later "fall away" in a time of testing (Luke 8:13), or fail to mature as other concerns choke out their faith (v. 14). By contrast, those who have genuine faith in Jesus will persevere in that faith, "hold[ing] . . . fast" to the gospel, and bearing fruit "with patience" (v. 15). Thankfully, Jesus prays for his own, so that our "faith may not fail" (22:32; see also John 17:1–12).

Personal Implications

Take time to reflect on the implications of Luke 7:1–9:50 for your own life today. Consider what you have learned that might lead you to praise God, repent of sin, and trust more deeply in his gracious promises. Make notes below on the personal implications for your walk with the Lord of the (1) *Gospel Glimpses*, (2) *Whole-Bible Connections*, (3) *Theological Soundings*, and (4) this passage as a whole.

1. Gospel Glimpses

2. Whole-Bible Connections

3. Theological Soundings

4. Luke 7:1–9:50

▶ As You Finish This Unit . . .

Take a moment now to ask for the Lord's blessing and help as you continue in this study of Luke. And take a moment also to look back through this unit of study, to reflect on some key things that the Lord may be teaching you—and perhaps to highlight and underline these things to review again in the future.

Definitions

[1] **Crucifixion** – A means of execution in which the person was fastened, by ropes or nails, to a crossbeam that was then raised and attached to a vertical beam, forming a cross. The process was designed to maximize pain and humiliation, and to serve as a deterrent for other potential offenders. Jesus suffered this form of execution not for any offense he had personally committed (Heb. 4:15) but as the atoning sacrifice for all who would believe in him (John 3:16).

[2] **Transfiguration** – An event in the life of Jesus Christ in which his physical appearance was transfigured, or changed, to reflect his heavenly glory as the Son of God.

[3] **Incarnation** – Literally "(becoming) in flesh," this term refers to God becoming a human being in the person of Jesus of Nazareth.

WEEK 6: THE JOURNEY OF THE KING, PART 1

Luke 9:51–13:21

▲

The Place of the Passage

In Luke 9:51 Jesus "set[s] his face to go to Jerusalem," opening what is known as Luke's journey narrative—a section of Luke's Gospel running through 19:27 and made up primarily of material found only in Luke. As he journeys toward the cross, Jesus challenges us to do two things: first, to reorient our vision of God, his character, and his priorities; and second, to live lives that reflect this new vision. In this early portion of the journey narrative, Jesus issues his two-fold challenge through his teachings about the kingdom of God, through his increasing conflict with Satan and with hypocritical leaders, and through his exhortations to prepare for future judgment.

The Big Picture

In Luke 9:51–13:21, Jesus reveals the true priorities of God's kingdom, engages in conflict with those who hinder those priorities, and urges us to prepare for coming judgment.

> ### Reflection and Discussion

Read through the complete passage for this study, Luke 9:51–13:21. Then review the questions below and write your notes on them concerning this section of Luke's Gospel. (For further background, see the *ESV Study Bible*, pages 1974–1985, or visit www.esvbible.org.)

1. Kingdom Priorities (9:51–11:13)

In Luke 9:62, Jesus declares that not all are "fit for the kingdom of God." According to this section of Luke, what priorities characterize those who *are* fit for the kingdom?

Martha is unable to focus on Jesus' teaching because she is distracted by many anxieties (Luke 10:41). According to 9:51–11:13, what false priorities might cause Jesus' followers anxiety? How do Jesus' teachings here set us free from such anxiety?

What does the parable of the good Samaritan, including Jesus' interaction with the scribe[1] who tests him, reveal about the nature of the kingdom of God? In other words, when God's reign is honored, what should life be like?

2. Kingdoms in Conflict (11:14–54)

In verses 29–32, Jesus mentions the "sign of Jonah," who was in the belly of a fish three days and nights just as Jesus would be in the earth three days and nights (Matt. 12:40). How does this contrast with the kind of "sign" that the crowds might have wanted to see Jesus perform? How does this contrast hint that Jesus' true power will be seen in his weakness?

In Luke 11:33–36, Jesus describes conflict between light and darkness. Based on the woes Jesus pronounces in verses 37–54, what are some indicators of a life that is "full of darkness"? By implication, what would a life "full of light" look like?

3. Preparing for Judgment (12:1–59)

In these verses, Jesus' teaching invites repentance through a sobering portrayal of the judgment that awaits us at our death (Luke 12:20) and at his return (v. 40). What details of the text make it clear that divine condemnation is something terrible, to be avoided at all costs? What details make it clear that God's people—that is, those who have genuine faith in Jesus—have nothing to fear?

What does Jesus want his followers to do now to "be ready" (Luke 12:40) for future judgment?

4. Judgment, Conflict, Kingdom (13:1–21)

These verses present the preceding themes in reverse order: preparing for judgment (through repentance), conflict (with Satan and with a hypocritical leader), and kingdom. According to Luke 13:1–9, who should prepare for the judgment to come, and in what ways?

Earlier, Jesus was accused of cooperating with Satan (Luke 11:15). According to 13:10–17, how are leaders who oppose Jesus furthering Satan's purposes?

How do the promises of kingdom power in Luke 13:18–21 encourage us as we strive to maintain the kingdom priorities revealed in 9:11–11:13?

Read through the following three sections on *Gospel Glimpses, Whole-Bible Connections*, and *Theological Soundings*. Then take time to consider the *Personal Implications* these sections may have for you.

Gospel Glimpses

TENDER LOVE FROM A HEAVENLY FATHER. Even as he announces the need to repent and prepare for judgment, Jesus stresses the tender love of God for his children. The Father gives spiritual insight to his "little children" (Luke 10:21); he hears our prayers (11:2), knows our needs (12:30), and gives us "good gifts" such as his Spirit (11:13) and kingdom (12:32); he even numbers the hairs of our head (12:7). In view of such love, we understand why Jesus can say to us, "Fear not" (vv. 7, 32)!

LOVE AS THE FRUIT OF LOVE. Some have understood the parable of the good Samaritan to teach salvation by works: if we will love our needy neighbors, we will "inherit eternal life" (Luke 10:25). Instead, three features of the parable demonstrate our need for the gift of salvation: (1) without a deep heart change, even knowing our duty will not motivate us to do it (v. 29); (2) Jesus calls for the kind of love that counts even an enemy as a neighbor, a mark of those transformed by God's mercy (6:27–36); and (3) Jesus speaks this parable as he journeys toward Jerusalem (9:51) to secure eternal life for us. Strength to love our neighbors is the fruit of the love God shows us in his Son.

Whole-Bible Connections

THE BLESSING OF THE NATIONS. In Luke 9:1–2, Jesus sends out 12 apostles— signaling his intention to fulfill God's purposes for Israel, which originally included 12 tribes (Gen. 49:28). In Luke 10:1, Jesus sends out 72 "others"— signaling his intention to fulfill God's purposes for the whole world, since the "table of nations"[2] in Genesis 10 contains 72 names. God's plan to bless "all the families of the earth" (Gen. 12:3) has become a reality in Jesus, whose "blood . . . ransomed people for God from every tribe and language and people and nation" (Rev. 5:9).

THE TWO GREATEST COMMANDMENTS. Jesus teaches that all of God's law is summarized in the commandments to love God and neighbor (Luke 10:27; Matt. 22:37–40; Mark 12:29–31; see also Rom. 13:9–10). The fact that both of these commandments are found in the Old Testament (Deut. 6:4–5; Lev. 19:18) demonstrates the unity of Scripture. Thus it is not true to say that the Old Testament is legalistic or "all about wrath." The New Testament certainly reveals new depths and dimensions of love (see John 13:34–35; 1 John 4:7–11, 19), but love for God and neighbor has always been at the heart of Scripture.

THE KINGDOM OF GOD. The concept of God's kingdom permeates all of Scripture. God exercises supreme rule over all of creation (Psalms 47; 93; 95; 145; Dan. 4:3, 34–35), so that life, righteousness, justice, and peace flourish where his reign is honored (Psalms 37; 85:9–13; 89:14; Isa. 9:7; Jer. 9:24; Hos. 2:19; Amos 5:24; Rom. 14:17). As Messiah, Jesus faithfully incarnates God's kingly rule in the present (Mark 1:15; Luke 11:20) and secures it for the future (John 3:5; 1 Cor. 6:9–11). At Jesus' return, all counterfeit kingdoms will be brought to an end (Psalm 46; Rev. 17:10–14), and God's people will rejoice in his everlasting rule (Rev. 11:15).

▶ Theological Soundings

FUTURE JUDGMENT. Jesus teaches that each person will be evaluated according to God's holy standards—first through an initial judgment that occurs at the moment of an individual's death (Luke 12:20; 16:22–23), and later through a final, universal judgment (10:12–15; 11:31–32; 12:4–9). Since only Jesus has lived a life of perfect love for God and neighbor, we can stand before God's judgment only if we are united to Jesus in genuine faith (12:8–9; 13:24–27). However, the deeds we have done will provide evidence that God's verdict is just: those whose lives bear the fruit of faith and repentance will inherit eternal life (12:35–48; 13:6–9).

SATAN'S REALITY—AND DEFEAT. Regarding Satan, two mistaken beliefs are common: first, that he does not exist; second, that he exists and is equal in power to God. Orthodox Christian faith affirms that Satan does indeed exist, but that he is a finite, fallen creature—more powerful than human beings (Luke 11:21, 24–26), but utterly defeated by Jesus (v. 22). Satan's power to enslave is no match for the redeeming power of our Savior (10:17–19; 13:10–17).

PRAYER AND GOD'S SOVEREIGNTY. Jesus never explains the mysterious relationship between God's sovereign rule and the role of prayer in shaping human history. But he teaches that God is a mighty King (Luke 11:2) who knows and controls all things (10:22; 12:2–7, 24, 28). Jesus also teaches that we may—indeed must—bring a whole range of requests to God in prayer (11:1–13). At the heart of this mystery is a loving Father-child relationship: God knows our needs (12:30), but he delights to hear us express our dependence on him and our gratitude for his grace (as even Jesus did; 10:21).

► **Personal Implications**

Take time to reflect on the implications of Luke 9:51–13:21 for your own life today. Consider what you have learned that might lead you to praise God, repent of sin, and trust more deeply in his gracious promises. Make notes below on the personal implications for your walk with the Lord of the (1) *Gospel Glimpses*, (2) *Whole-Bible Connections*, (3) *Theological Soundings*, and (4) this passage as a whole.

1. Gospel Glimpses

2. Whole-Bible Connections

3. Theological Soundings

4. Luke 9:51–13:21

49

As You Finish This Unit . . .

Take a moment now to ask for the Lord's blessing and help as you continue in this study of Luke. And take a moment also to look back through this unit of study, to reflect on some key things that the Lord may be teaching you—and perhaps to highlight and underline these things to review again in the future.

Definitions

[1] **Scribe** – Someone trained and authorized to transcribe, teach, and interpret the Scriptures. Jesus often criticized scribes for their pride, their legalistic approach to the Scriptures, and their refusal to believe in him.

[2] **Table of nations** – The Genesis 10 list of the descendants of Shem, Ham, and Japheth, from whom all the nations of the earth are descended.

Week 7: The Journey of the King, Part 2

Luke 13:22–17:10

▲

Luke 13:22 reminds us that Jesus is still "journeying toward Jerusalem," and therefore toward his death and resurrection. From this point through 17:11 (where we read a third and final description of Jesus' progress toward Jerusalem), Jesus continues to reshape our vision of God and of a God-honoring life. He does this by calling us to embrace the "inside-out" priorities of God's kingdom, to commit to the radical demands of discipleship, and to repent, especially of idolatrous love of wealth. Alongside such teaching Jesus highlights our deep need—and God's extravagant supply—of saving grace.

The Big Picture

Luke 13:22–17:10 confronts us with priorities for kingdom life that are more extreme, and images of God's grace that are more lavish, than the human heart can fathom.

▶ Reflection and Discussion

Read through the complete passage for this study, Luke 13:22–17:10. Then review the questions below and write your notes on them concerning this section of Luke's Gospel. (For further background, see the *ESV Study Bible*, pages 1985–1992, or visit esv.org.)

1. The Last Will Be First (13:22–14:24)

This section of Luke's Gospel emphasizes two patterns of reversal—one involving a first/last interchange (Luke 13:30), and another a pattern of humiliation/exaltation (14:11). For whom are these patterns intended as warnings or rebukes? Who should hear these patterns as encouragements or as commendations?

What specific commands does Jesus give to indicate how we should respond to these patterns?

When Jesus is warned to flee Herod Antipas, his reply is paradoxical: he will leave Herod's territory, but this will only lead him closer to death (Luke 13:31–35). How does Jesus' destiny in Jerusalem exemplify the first/last and humiliation/exaltation patterns?

2. Radical Demands, Radical Grace (14:25–15:32)

In your own words, how would you summarize the demands Luke 14:25–35 places on those who follow Jesus? What is the significance of the fact that Jesus speaks these words to "great crowds"?

What indicates that the Pharisees[1] and scribes of Luke 15:1–2 are unwilling to count the cost of discipleship? What factors make them reluctant to do so?

What specific features of the parables in Luke 15:3–32 indicate the radical nature of God's grace? How does this grace make us willing to meet the costly demands of discipleship?

3. Of Riches and Repentance (16:1–31)

According to these verses, what patterns in our lives might indicate whether we are serving God or money as our master? What does it mean to use money to "make friends" for ourselves (Luke 16:9) rather than to "exalt" ourselves "among men" (v. 15)?

Luke 16:16–17 affirms that Jesus' coming has not invalidated the Old Testament law. How is this truth illustrated by the conclusion of the parable of the rich man and Lazarus (vv. 27–31)?

4. Radical Demands, Radical Need (17:1–10)

What two radical demands does Jesus make in Luke 17:1–4? According to verses 5–6, what is necessary if we are to meet such demands?

How does Luke 17:7–10 indicate our need for God's grace—and how does recognizing such need strengthen our faith?

Read through the following three sections on *Gospel Glimpses*, *Whole-Bible Connections*, and *Theological Soundings*. Then take time to consider the *Personal Implications* these sections may have for you.

Gospel Glimpses

GRACE VERSUS MERIT. Luke 17:1–10 highlights God's grace by making it clear that even perfect obedience does not merit his favor. If we did everything God requires of us, including never tempting anyone to sin (vv. 1–2) and perfectly forgiving others (vv. 3–4), our obedience would not obligate God in any way (vv. 7–10). By implication, any blessing we receive from God is a gift of grace; this is true even when God promises blessing in response to our obedience (as in 14:10–14). Free grace, secured by Jesus' work, is the only basis for God's goodness to sinners.

MERCY FOR THE NEEDY. Jesus' words and deeds contrast self-reliance with dependence on mercy: guests at a banquet vie for honor, while Jesus heals a man disfigured by disease (Luke 14:1–11); the host invites wealthy friends and family, when he should invite "the poor, the crippled, the lame, the blind" (v. 13; compare v. 21); a pitiless rich man endures torment, while a beggar "is comforted" (16:19–31). Jesus is teaching us a twofold lesson: first, deep desire for saving mercy is fueled by recognition of our desperate need; second, receiving such mercy will make us eager to serve, rather than neglect, others in need.

THE PRODIGAL FATHER. The real scandal of the parable of the prodigal son (Luke 15:11–32) is the excess with which the father, representing God, lavishes love on his younger son. But according to Jesus, the God of heaven delights to run to us (v. 20), to bestow on us the status of sons and daughters (v. 22), and to compromise his own dignity in order to enhance ours. In Jesus, this God endures not only angry criticism (see vv. 2, 28–30) but torment and death—all in order to shower love on anyone who will repent and rest in his mercy.

Whole-Bible Connections

THE MESSIANIC BANQUET. Jesus often portrays the joys of eternal life through the image of feasting (Luke 12:35–37; 13:29; 14:8, 15–24; 15:23; 22:30; see also Matt. 5:6; 22:1–14; 25:10). Such imagery draws on the Old Testament, where sacred meals signify fellowship with God (Ex. 24:11; Deut. 27:7) and enjoyment of his blessings (Leviticus 23; Deut. 16:10–17). Isaiah depicts the fulfillment of these blessings as a feast at which God will destroy death (Isa. 25:6–9); in Revelation, a similar scene is described as "the marriage supper of the Lamb"

(Rev. 19:6–9). Jesus invites us to anticipate this great banquet through the celebration of the Lord's Supper (Luke 22:14–20).

CONTINUITY OF OLD AND NEW. This section of Luke repeatedly indicates that God's dealings with the world in the New Testament era are consistent with his work in the Old Testament era: "Abraham and Isaac and Jacob" are citizens of the kingdom Jesus brings (Luke 13:28); "Moses and the Prophets" provide sufficient testimony to bring sinners to repentance (16:29); Jesus stands in a long line of prophets who have died in Jerusalem (13:34). Though Jesus' coming represents a significant change in the outworking of God's kingdom (16:16), his work fulfills, rather than destroys, the purposes, promises, and patterns of action revealed in the Old Testament.

▶ Theological Soundings

BIBLICAL UNIVERSALISM.[2] The doctrine of universalism contradicts Jesus' teaching about the final judgment of the fate of the unrepentant (Luke 13:28; 14:24; 16:25–26). However, Jesus does command the church to summon all kinds of people to repentance and faith—whether rich or poor, sinful or self-righteous, Jewish or Gentile (13:29–30; 14:21–23). Though not everyone will enter the "narrow door" of genuine faith in Christ (13:24–27), many "from east and west, and from north and south" will (v. 29). Rejection of a false doctrine of universalism should not dampen proper biblical zeal to see God's house "filled" (14:23).

THE RESURRECTION. Christian doctrine affirms not only the resurrection of Christ but also a general resurrection in which, at Christ's second coming, the bodies and souls of the deceased will be reunited. (Those who are alive at Christ's return will receive resurrection bodies, though they have not experienced death; see 1 Cor. 15:51–53.) Some will be raised "to everlasting life" and others "to shame and everlasting contempt" (Dan. 12:2). Jesus views the future glory of the "resurrection of the just" (Luke 14:14) as greater than any glory we could secure for ourselves in the present, and therefore as a motive for loving those who have nothing to offer us in return.

THE INTERMEDIATE STATE. Before Christ returns to carry out final judgment, the souls of those who die will enter into what is known as the "intermediate state"—an experience of blessedness in God's presence for the faithful (heaven) and of punishment apart from him for the unbelieving (hell). While not all of its details should be pressed for doctrinal significance, Jesus' parable of the rich man and Lazarus (Luke 16:19–31) is foundational to our understanding of this interim state. The parable offers comfort to those who endure affliction now, and an urgent warning to those who refuse the biblical call to repent, for "none may cross from there [hell] to us [in heaven]" (v. 26).

▶ **Personal Implications**

Take time to reflect on the implications of Luke 13:22–17:10 for your own life today. Consider what you have learned that might lead you to praise God, repent of sin, and trust more deeply in his gracious promises. Make notes below on the personal implications for your walk with the Lord of the (1) *Gospel Glimpses*, (2) *Whole-Bible Connections*, (3) *Theological Soundings*, and (4) this passage as a whole.

1. Gospel Glimpses

2. Whole-Bible Connections

3. Theological Soundings

4. Luke 13:22–17:10

As You Finish This Unit . . .

Take a moment now to ask for the Lord's blessing and help as you continue in this study of Luke. And take a moment also to look back through this unit of study, to reflect on some key things that the Lord may be teaching you—and perhaps to highlight and underline these things to review again in the future.

Definitions

[1] **Pharisee** – A member of a popular religious/political party in NT times characterized by strict adherence to the law of Moses and also to extrabiblical Jewish traditions. The Pharisees were frequently criticized by Jesus for their legalistic and hypocritical practices.

[2] **Universalism** – The unbiblical belief that all people will be saved from eternal damnation, regardless of whether or not they come to faith in Christ.

WEEK 8: THE JOURNEY OF THE KING, PART 3

Luke 17:11–19:27

The Place of the Passage

Opening with a third reminder of Jesus' progress toward Jerusalem (Luke 17:11), this section concludes Luke's journey narrative, once again calling us to radically refashion our lives in light of God's character and kingdom priorities. Major themes of Jesus' teaching here include readiness for his second coming, the dangers of idolatry and self-righteousness, and the nature and effects of saving faith. The urgency of Jesus' message is heightened by tension: though Jesus has come "to seek and to save the lost" (19:10), when he reaches Jerusalem he will be put to death by those who reject their true King and the salvation he brings (18:31–33; 19:14).

The Big Picture

Luke 17:11–19:27 calls us to repentance and faith by contrasting the joy of those who embrace Jesus with the misery of those who reject him.

Reflection and Discussion

Read through the complete passage for this study, Luke 17:11–19:27. Then review the questions below and write your notes on them concerning this section of Luke's Gospel. (For further background, see the *ESV Study Bible*, pages 1993–1998, or visit esv.org.)

1. Mercy and Gratitude (17:11–19)

While 10 lepers ask Jesus to "have mercy" on them, Jesus commends only one—a Samaritan. According to this story, what attitudes provide evidence of true faith?

2. The Coming of the Kingdom (17:20–18:8)

In Luke 17:22–37, what do Jesus' illustrations from nature (lightning flashing, vultures gathering) and from Scripture (Noah, Lot) teach us about his return?

Luke 18:1 suggests that we might "lose heart" as we await Jesus' second coming. What realities described in 17:17–18:8 might cause us to lose heart? How does Jesus' parable in 18:1–8 keep us from doing so?

3. Kingdom Humility (18:9–17)

In Luke 18:9, self-righteousness[1] and contempt for others go hand in hand. How is this link demonstrated by Jesus' parable in verses 10–14? How does the disciples' behavior in verse 15 give evidence of a similar pattern?

Based on Luke 18:10–17, how might we combat self-righteousness in our own hearts?

4. Leaving All to Follow the King (18:18–34)

The rich ruler who approaches Jesus is prepared to "do" a great deal (Luke 18:18); why is he unwilling to do the one thing Jesus asks of him? What is it about wealth that makes it such a powerful idol?

Jesus calls his disciples to embrace a pattern of present suffering followed by future blessing (Luke 18:28–30)—a pattern that characterizes Jesus' life as well (vv. 31–33). How does knowing that we share this pattern with Jesus strengthen us to fight against the power of idols?

5. Persistent Faith, True Repentance (18:35–19:10)

How do the blind beggar and Zacchaeus overcome obstacles that are keeping them from Jesus? What does this teach us about the nature of faith?

What points of contrast do you see between Zacchaeus and the rich ruler of Luke 18:18–23?

6. About the Master's Business (19:11–27)

The parable of the 10 minas[2] suggests that servants who know their master's character will delight to be about his business. What features of Luke 17:11–19:27 demonstrate that our Master, Jesus, is gracious and compassionate rather than "severe"?

Read through the following three sections on *Gospel Glimpses*, *Whole-Bible Connections*, and *Theological Soundings*. Then take time to consider the *Personal Implications* these sections may have for you.

▶ Gospel Glimpses

SEEKING AND SAVING THE LOST. In this section of Luke's Gospel, Jesus repeatedly extends the blessings of salvation to those who are despised and treated "with contempt" (Luke 18:9)—including a Samaritan, children, a blind beggar, and Zacchaeus the tax collector. Unlike the Pharisee in his parable (vv. 10–14), Jesus embraces sinners who seek God's mercy. The Son of Man delights "to seek and to save the lost" (19:10)—even if it means being treated with contempt for our sake (18:32–33; 19:14).

DEEP FAITH, TRUE FRUIT. Faith that is born from a profound sense of sin, and thus from deep appreciation for God's mercy, will lead us to costly repentance and obedience. This is the message we learn through two tax collectors—one a sinner pleading for mercy in Jesus' parable (Luke 18:9–14), and the other a repentant Zacchaeus (19:1–10). By contrast, the Pharisee of Jesus' parable and the rich ruler of 18:18–23 boldly claim to obey God but are enslaved to the idols of pride and riches. Self-righteousness will never produce true repentance and obedience. These fruits grow only where seeds of desperate need are planted in the soil of God's unmerited favor to sinners.

▶ Whole-Bible Connections

THE SON OF MAN. In Psalm 8:4, "the son of man" is a designation for humanity as a whole, given dominion over the earth at creation. In Daniel 7:13–14, the "son of man" is a glorious figure to whom God gives "an everlasting dominion," and who (like God) is to be honored and served by "all peoples." Jesus' use of the title (Luke 17:22; 19:10) is therefore a claim to be a divine-human mediator who faithfully exercises dominion over all things—even death (Heb. 2:6–9). The Son of Man exercises this dominion through his suffering (Luke 17:25; 18:31–33), his exaltation (Acts 7:56; Rev. 1:13), and his return to judge the earth (Luke 17:24, 30; 18:8; Rev. 14:14).

JUDGMENT—AND DELIVERANCE. In the days of Noah (Gen. 6:5–9:17) and of Lot (Gen. 18:20–19:29), God's judgment fell decisively on human wickedness. Throughout Scripture, these events represent both devastating judgment (Isa. 13:19; Lam. 4:6; Amos 4:11; 2 Pet. 2:5–9; Jude 7) and God's commitment to provide a means of escape for his people (Heb. 11:7; 1 Pet. 3:20; 2 Pet. 2:9). The effect is always to call sinners to repentance so that they might experience God's faithful love rather than his anger (Deut. 29:22–30:3; Isa. 1:9–20; 54:7–10). When Jesus compares his return to "the days of Noah" and "of Lot" (Luke 17:26–30), he is warning us of coming judgment—and assuring us that he is God's appointed means of rescue.

Theological Soundings

JUSTIFICATION[3] BY FAITH. In Jesus' parable of the Pharisee and the tax collector (Luke 18:9–14) we see three principles that are at the heart of the doctrine of justification: (1) boasting in human works—even religious disciplines—is worthless before God; (2) our only hope is to confess our need as sinners, casting ourselves on God's mercy; and (3) the issue is not where we stand in comparison to others, but whether we are accepted by God. (The Greek term for "be merciful" even implies securing mercy through the proper means, so that verse 13 may allude to trust in the death of a sacrificial substitute.) Though we often associate it with the apostle Paul (Rom. 3:20–5:1; Gal. 2:16; 3:1–14), the doctrine of justification by faith clearly has its roots in Jesus' teaching, in such passages as this one.

THE SECOND COMING OF CHRIST. The Christian church has always acknowledged that Jesus, now enthroned in heaven, will one day return to the earth. Jesus repeatedly emphasizes this truth in Luke 17:11–19:27. He even indicates that, as the returning Lord, he will be the same person who died and rose again for our salvation (17:22–25; 18:31–33). Therefore we look forward to his return in confident hope, though many details surrounding it (such as its timing: 17:20; 19:11) remain mysterious to us.

NOW AND NOT YET. Much of Christian doctrine involves a tension between the "now" and the "not yet." The kingdom of God, for example, is already "in [our] midst" (Luke 17:21) and can be "receive[d]" now (18:17); yet the kingdom will enter a new phase at Jesus' return (19:12–15), so that we will "enter it" later (18:17, 24–25). Similarly, eternal life is something that will be inherited "in the age to come" (18:30; see also v. 18), but many aspects of it can be experienced now (18:14; 19:9). When we see powerful signs of God's saving work in our hearts and in our world, but long to see that work brought to completion, we are experiencing a tension that is a fundamental feature of Jesus' teaching, and therefore of Christian life and belief.

Personal Implications

Take time to reflect on the implications of Luke 17:11–19:27 for your own life today. Consider what you have learned that might lead you to praise God, repent of sin, and trust more deeply in his gracious promises. Make notes below on the personal implications for your walk with the Lord of the (1) *Gospel Glimpses*, (2) *Whole-Bible Connections*, (3) *Theological Soundings*, and (4) this passage as a whole.

1. Gospel Glimpses

2. Whole-Bible Connections

3. Theological Soundings

4. Luke 17:11–19:27

As You Finish This Unit . . .

Take a moment now to ask for the Lord's blessing and help as you continue in this study of Luke. And take a moment also to look back through this unit of study, to reflect on some key things that the Lord may be teaching you—and perhaps to highlight and underline these things to review again in the future.

Definitions

[1] **Self-righteousness** – The belief that one is acceptable before God because of one's own moral uprightness or human effort, rather than depending on the grace of God. Self-righteousness begins with evaluating oneself in light of human standards rather than God's standards, and is therefore typically accompanied by pride and a judgmental attitude toward others.

[2] **Mina** – A unit of measurement for money, roughly equivalent to 1.25 pounds. A mina of silver was worth about three months' wages for a first-century laborer. Jesus' parable of the 10 minas is distinct from, but closely related to, the parable of the talents (Matt. 25:14–30).

[3] **Justification** – The act of God's grace in bringing sinners into a new covenant relationship with himself and counting them as righteous before him through the forgiveness of their sins (Rom. 3:20–26).

Week 9: The Tragic Triumph of Jesus' Jerusalem Ministry

Luke 19:28–21:38

▲

The Place of the Passage

Like every Gospel writer, Luke gives a detailed account of the final week leading up to Jesus' death. Luke 19:28–21:38 records events occurring on what we would call Sunday through Thursday of this week: Jesus' entry into Jerusalem and his subsequent ministry centered on the temple. At times this section emphasizes themes of triumph and joy, as the arrival of God's anointed King brings the fulfillment of God's redeeming promises nearer. At other times, the section sounds notes of sorrow, since Jesus experiences rejection that will lead not only to his death but also to divine judgment on Jerusalem itself. Though the tone of the section varies, its consistent purpose is to demonstrate that Jesus is the chosen Redeemer who brings all of Scripture's promises to fulfillment.

The Big Picture

Luke 19:28–21:38 recounts Jesus' triumphant yet tragic ministry in Jerusalem, calling us to trust Jesus as God's anointed Savior-King.

▶ Reflection and Discussion

Read through the complete passage for this study, Luke 19:28–21:38. Then review the questions below and write your notes on them concerning this section of Luke's Gospel. (For further background, see the *ESV Study Bible*, pages 1998–2004, or visit esv.org.)

1. Triumph and Tragedy (19:28–48)

As Jesus enters Jerusalem, Luke emphasizes the joyful response of his disciples. What details of Luke 19:28–38 represent appropriate ways for disciples to honor God's anointed King?

Jesus shatters the mood of celebration by predicting the destruction of Jerusalem and enacting judgment on the temple. How do Isaiah 56:3–8 and Jeremiah 7:1–11—texts that stand behind Luke 19:46—shed light on the reasons behind the judgment Jesus brings?

2. Jesus Answers—and Issues—Challenges (20:1–21:4)

In Luke 20:1–44, Jesus responds with remarkable wisdom to several attempts to entrap him. What features of Jesus' responses represent shrewd practical judgment?

Jesus also challenges his opponents with biblical reasoning. What biblical principle lies behind Jesus' logic in Luke 20:24–25? What biblical truth have the Sadducees[1] missed, according to verses 37–38?

Jesus goes on the offensive in Luke 20:45–21:4. How does his commendation of the widow's offering function as a critique of the scribes? How does it remind us not to confuse human wisdom (as embodied by Jesus' opponents) with God's wisdom (as embodied by Jesus)?

3. Judgment in This Age and the Next (21:5–38)

Here Jesus gives more detailed teaching about two events: the destruction of Jerusalem (Luke 19:43–44) and his second coming (9:26; 17:22–37). According to 21:5–24, what things must take place before "the end"—that is, before Christ's return? (Note that some of these "things" are ongoing even today, while some occurred with the Romans' destruction of Jerusalem in AD 70.)

According to Luke 21:25–27, what kinds of events will be associated with Jesus' return?

What should followers of Jesus do to prepare for coming judgment (Luke 21:34–36)?

_____

_____

_____

_____

_____

_____

Read through the following three sections on *Gospel Glimpses*, *Whole-Bible Connections*, and *Theological Soundings*. Then take time to consider the *Personal Implications* these sections may have for you.

▶ Gospel Glimpses

THE HUMBLE KING. Jesus arrives in Jerusalem in the manner foretold by the prophet Zechariah: "Behold, your king is coming to you ... humble and mounted on a donkey, on a colt, the foal of a donkey" (Zech. 9:9). The humble king is also a weeping judge, shedding tears over unrepentant Jerusalem (Luke 19:41–44). Only in Jesus do we see royal power and authority perfectly combined with humility and compassion. We may trust him to perform radical spiritual surgery in our lives because he is mighty enough to destroy our sin, yet merciful enough to save our souls.

PATIENT, COSTLY LOVE. One of the lessons taught by Jesus' parable of the wicked tenants (Luke 20:9–18) is God's patient, costly love for sinners. God, depicted as a vineyard owner, has every right to destroy his people when we reject prophets and other leaders who call us to faithfulness (v. 10). Instead, he patiently reaches out to us again and again (vv. 11–12). While justice demands that we pay the price for our sins, God pays an even greater price—ultimately sending his "beloved son" to die (vv. 13–15). Surely our response to such love should be repentant, joyful thanksgiving!

▶ Whole-Bible Connections

JESUS FULFILLS THE SCRIPTURES. Jesus' ministry in Jerusalem emphasizes his fulfillment of the Old Testament Scriptures. He is the humble king (Zech.

9:9) who "comes in the name of the Lord" (Luke 19:38; Ps. 118:26), the rejected cornerstone (Luke 20:17; Ps. 118:22), the greater "Lord" of whom David spoke (Luke 20:41–43; Ps. 110:1), and one whose resurrection will fulfill a promise that goes back as far as Moses and even Abraham (Luke 20:37). God's purpose to redeem his people is attested throughout the Scriptures—all of which are brought to completion in Jesus.

THE REJECTED REDEEMER. As the rejected cornerstone (Luke 20:17), Jesus represents the culmination of a larger biblical pattern in which God raises up leaders who are then scorned by his people (vv. 10–12). Acts 7:1–53 reminds us that two of the Old Testament's greatest heroes were rejected by their fellow Israelites: Joseph was sold into slavery, and later he delivered Israel from famine; Moses became an exile from Egypt, then returned to free the nation from slavery. This pattern is intensified in Jesus: although he was crucified by "sinful men" (Luke 24:7), God has now "exalted him . . . as Leader and Savior, to give repentance to Israel and forgiveness of sins" (Acts 5:31).

"THE LORD SAID TO MY LORD." Proclaiming the promise of a greater son of David who would reign forever (2 Sam. 7:12–16), Psalm 110 envisions a king who is enthroned at God's right hand, whose enemies are put under his feet by God, and who is also an eternal priest. Following logic first employed by Jesus (Luke 20:41–44), New Testament writers argue from this psalm that Jesus is greater than David (Acts 2:32–35), angels (Heb. 1:13), and Old Testament priests (Heb. 6:19–7:17). Because Jesus is enthroned at God's "right hand," with all authorities beneath his feet (Eph. 1:20–23; 1 Pet. 3:22), his people have nothing to fear (Rom. 8:34; Heb. 10:12–13). Ultimately, even death, our final enemy, will be put under the feet of our Savior-King (1 Cor. 15:25–26).

▶ **Theological Soundings**

THE INSPIRATION OF SCRIPTURE. The doctrine of inspiration affirms that the Holy Spirit caused biblical authors to express God's truth in human language. This work of inspiration extends to every part of Scripture, including its very words. In Luke 20:37–38, Jesus defends the doctrine of the resurrection based on the grammar of Exodus 3:6 ("I am [rather than 'I was'] the God of Abraham"). In Luke 20:41–44 Jesus challenges his opponents' beliefs about the Messiah based on a single word from Psalm 110:1 ("my Lord," one word in Hebrew). Jesus' willingness to base important theological arguments on the details of the biblical text calls us to receive all of Scripture as God's inspired Word.

PERSEVERANCE[2] AND PRESERVATION.[3] Jesus' teaching about future judgment in Luke 21 stresses both our duty to remain faithful (perseverance) and God's gracious provision of the strength that enables us to do so

71

(preservation). We must guard our hearts against distractions as we await Jesus' return (v. 34), and we must pray vigilantly (v. 36a); but it is God who will give us "strength to escape" the trials of the last days and "to stand" in the day of judgment (v. 36b). "Fear and . . . foreboding" may make it difficult to endure (v. 26), but Jesus sustains us with the promise that our "redemption is drawing near" (v. 28). Our ability to persevere is rooted in the divine work of preservation.

Personal Implications

Take time to reflect on the implications of Luke 19:28–21:38 for your own life today. Consider what you have learned that might lead you to praise God, repent of sin, and trust more deeply in his gracious promises. Make notes below on the personal implications for your walk with the Lord of the (1) *Gospel Glimpses*, (2) *Whole-Bible Connections*, (3) *Theological Soundings*, and (4) this passage as a whole.

1. Gospel Glimpses

2. Whole-Bible Connections

3. Theological Soundings

4. Luke 19:28–21:38

Take a moment now to ask for the Lord's blessing and help as you continue in this study of Luke. And take a moment also to look back through this unit of study, to reflect on some key things that the Lord may be teaching you—and perhaps to highlight and underline these things to review again in the future.

Definitions

[1] **Sadducee** – A member of a religious/political party during Jesus' time characterized by (1) rejection of any OT writings except Genesis—Deuteronomy, (2) rejection of belief in the resurrection and in angels and demons, (3) an interest in Greek culture and beliefs, and (4) affluence, as a result of their influential priestly positions.

[2] **Perseverance of the saints** – According to this doctrine, all true believers will remain faithful to the end. Those who willfully continue in sin, or relapse into sin, thereby reveal that they were never truly believers. Others may for a time *appear* to abandon their faith, though they have not in fact done so. This doctrine does not deny the reality that even true believers still sin, nor does it mean that those who have made a profession of faith are free to live sinful, godless lives.

[3] **Preservation** – Related to perseverance of the saints, this doctrine affirms that it is God who enables true believers to remain faithful. God's work of preservation warns us against pride and presumption, calling us instead to humble dependence on God's sustaining grace.

WEEK 10: THE DEATH
OF GOD'S SON

Luke 22:1–23:56

▲

The Place of the Passage

Jesus' death and resurrection are the climactic events of his ministry, and therefore of Luke's Gospel. In chapters 22–23, Luke depicts Jesus' betrayal, arrest, trials, crucifixion, and death, with special attention to three themes. First, Jesus dies as an innocent sacrifice, not suffering for any sin he has committed. Second, Jesus' death accomplishes God's saving purposes as expressed in various Old Testament prophecies and patterns. Finally, Jesus is the Son of God who remains faithful to his Father, even to his dying breath. Together these themes call us to entrust ourselves entirely to Jesus, who delivers us from condemnation and death by enduring them in our place.

The Big Picture

Through a detailed account of Jesus' crucifixion and the events leading up to it, Luke 22–23 calls us to trust the Son of God who died to save us while refusing to save himself.

75

Reflection and Discussion

Read through the complete passage for this study, Luke 22–23. Then review the questions below and write your notes on them concerning this section of Luke's Gospel. (For further background, see the *ESV Study Bible*, pages 2004–2012, or visit esv.org.)

1. The Significance of Jesus' Death (22:1–22)

In this text, Jesus portrays his death as the center point of God's saving work. In what ways does he look backward, calling us to see his death as the fulfillment of Old Testament realities?

In what ways does Jesus look forward, suggesting that his death is essential for the future life and blessing of God's people?

2. Preparing for Coming Trials (22:23–65)

According to Luke 22:23–46, what kinds of temptations and trials confront Jesus' disciples as his betrayal and arrest grows near?

What instruction and encouragement does Jesus offer, whether by word or example, to prepare his disciples to face these trials?

At Gethsemane, Jesus asks the Father for strength to go willingly to his death. What evidence from Luke 22:43–65 indicates that God has answered Jesus' prayer?

3. Jesus Is Tried, Found Innocent—and Condemned (22:66–23:25)

In these verses, what accusations are brought against Jesus by his opponents?

In what ways do these accusations reflect truth (even if it is misunderstood by Jesus' accusers)? In what ways are these accusations simply false?

4. The Death of the Son of God (23:26–56)

In Luke 23:26–43, how does Jesus demonstrate concern for other people? What response would you expect in these circumstances from an ordinary human being?

How do the similarities between Luke 23:35–39 and 4:3–13 suggest that the cross is the "opportune time" (v. 13) for Satan's final temptation of Jesus? In what ways is this final temptation more severe than the earlier wilderness temptation?

Many in the first century would have seen Jesus' crucifixion, which represented a divine curse (see Deut. 21:22–23; Gal. 3:13), as grounds to reject him. How should we respond to Jesus instead, based on Luke's descriptions of the repentant criminal (Luke 23:41–43), the centurion (v. 47), and Joseph of Arimathea (vv. 50–51)?

Read through the following three sections on *Gospel Glimpses*, *Whole-Bible Connections*, and *Theological Soundings*. Then take time to consider the *Personal Implications* these sections may have for you.

► Gospel Glimpses

"HE SAVED OTHERS." On the cross, Jesus is mocked with the challenge, "He saved others; let him save himself" (Luke 23:35). By contrast, Luke highlights Jesus' care for others, even as he goes to his death. Jesus expresses concern for the trials facing his disciples (22:31–32) and the "daughters of Jerusalem" (23:28–31), heals one who has come to arrest him (22:50–51), and promises salvation to a repentant criminal (23:43). Jesus even asks God to forgive those who crucify him (23:34). This is the beauty of the gospel: rather than saving himself, Jesus sacrifices himself for our salvation and, never lapsing into self-pity, loves others to the end.

THE CUP AND THE CROSS. Jesus' redeeming love is magnified when we understand his prayer that the Father would "remove this cup" from him (Luke 22:42). Scripture often portrays God's wrath as a cup filled with wine (Ps. 75:8; Isa. 51:17–23; 63:6; Rev. 14:19; 16:19); when poured out in judgment, it causes unbearable anguish (Jer. 25:15–27; Rev. 14:10–11). At the cross, Jesus drained this cup on behalf of anyone who puts their trust in him. How glorious is the grace that leads the Father to send his Son to bear such wrath in our place! How wondrous is the love that leads the Son to endure such agony for us!

THE FATHER'S GOODNESS. Jesus' prayers in Luke 22–23 show us that we can trust God's goodness even in the worst circumstances imaginable. When he needs strength to drink the cup of wrath, Jesus cries out to his Father (Luke 22:42). On the cross, still confident in God's mercy, Jesus asks the Father to forgive the soldiers who are crucifying him (23:34). Even at the moment of his death, when all outward signs of God's favor have vanished, Jesus entrusts his spirit to his Father's hands (23:46). If God's gracious care is sufficient for such trials, there is never a time when we are beyond its reach.

► Whole-Bible Connections

THE SACRIFICE THAT SEALS A NEW COVENANT.[1] At the Last Supper, Jesus refers to the cup shared with his disciples as "the new covenant in my blood" (Luke 22:20; 1 Cor. 11:25). God's single plan to redeem his fallen world has unfolded in history through a series of covenants established with various mediators,[2] with each covenant advancing God's purpose toward its ultimate fulfillment in the new covenant (Jer. 31:31–34), also known as the "everlasting covenant" (Isa. 55:3; Jer. 32:40; Ezek. 37:26). Jesus is the second Adam (1 Cor. 15:45, 47), the true Seed of Abraham (Gal. 3:16), the Prophet greater than Moses (Heb. 3:1–6; compare Acts 3:22), and the Son of David (Matt. 1:1)—in short, he is the Mediator of the new covenant, to which all others have pointed. And as previous covenants were sealed through animal sacrifice (see Gen. 8:20;

15:7–17; Heb. 9:18–22), the new covenant is sealed with the most precious blood of all—that of the Son of God (Heb. 9:12–14; 10:10–19).

OPENING THE WAY TO PARADISE. Luke 23:35–43 continues the "second Adam" theme introduced in Luke 4:1–13. Not only does the crucified Jesus remain faithful to God despite being challenged three times to save himself, but he also promises the repentant criminal a place in "Paradise" (23:43). In the Greek Old Testament, this word refers to the garden of Eden, where life flourishes (Isa. 51:3; Ezek. 36:35); in the New Testament, it signifies intimate knowledge of God (2 Cor. 12:3–4) and complete victory over death (Rev. 2:7). While the failure of the first Adam closed the way to Eden (Gen. 3:23–24), the faithfulness of the second Adam reopens the way to perfect fellowship with God, beginning "today" (Luke 23:43) and lasting forever in the "new heaven and . . . new earth" (Rev. 21:1).

Theological Soundings

SUBSTITUTIONARY ATONEMENT. The church has always looked to Jesus' death as an act of substitutionary atonement: Jesus endures in our place (i.e., as a substitute) the judgment we deserve; this is the means by which our forgiveness is secured (atonement). Luke emphasizes this truth in three ways: (1) as the Passover lamb died to spare Israel's firstborn (Ex. 12:21–27), Jesus dies for his people (Luke 22:19); (2) Jesus drinks the cup of God's wrath (22:42), so his death is an outpouring of God's judgment; and (3) because Jesus dies an innocent man (22:37; 23:22, 41, 47), the judgment he endures is that due to our sin, not to any sin of his own.

THE REALITY OF JESUS' DEATH. In order for Jesus' death to have any atoning significance for flesh-and-blood creatures, it must be a historical and physical reality. Thus Christian theology denies suggestions that Jesus only appeared to have a physical body (an ancient heresy known as Docetism) or that he only appeared to die. Various details of Luke 22–23 affirm the reality of Jesus' death: Jesus refers to his own body and blood (22:19–20); he sweats (22:44); he is beaten and struck (vv. 63–64); he has a body that can be clothed (23:11), stripped naked (v. 34), nailed to a cross (v. 33), carefully prepared for burial, and laid to rest (v. 53). Jesus' death certainly has more spiritual significance than any other person's, but it is no less real.

Personal Implications

Take time to reflect on the implications of Luke 22–23 for your own life today. Consider what you have learned that might lead you to praise God, repent of sin, and trust more deeply in his gracious promises. Make notes below on the personal implications for your walk with the Lord of the (1) *Gospel Glimpses*, (2) *Whole-Bible Connections*, (3) *Theological Soundings*, and (4) this passage as a whole.

1. Gospel Glimpses

2. Whole-Bible Connections

3. Theological Soundings

4. Luke 22–23

▶ **As You Finish This Unit . . .**

Take a moment now to ask for the Lord's blessing and help as you continue in this study of Luke. And take a moment also to look back through this unit of study, to reflect on some key things that the Lord may be teaching you—and perhaps to highlight and underline these things to review again in the future.

Definitions

[1] **Covenant** – A binding agreement between two parties, typically involving a formal statement of their relationship, a list of stipulations and obligations for both parties, a list of witnesses to the agreement, and a list of curses for unfaithfulness and blessings for faithfulness to the agreement. The Old Testament is more properly understood as the old covenant, meaning the agreement God established between himself and his people prior to the coming of Jesus Christ and its replacement by the new covenant (New Testament).

[2] **Mediator** – One who intercedes between parties to resolve a conflict or achieve a goal, such as the carrying out of a covenant. Jesus is the Mediator between God and rebellious humanity (1 Tim. 2:5; compare Heb. 9:15; 12:24).

Week 11: The Resurrection of God's Son

Luke 24:1–53

The Place of the Passage

Though it constitutes only one chapter, several factors place Luke's account of Jesus' resurrection among the most significant portions of his Gospel. First, the historical reality of Jesus' resurrection proves, despite the shame associated with crucifixion, that God is pleased with Jesus' work as redeemer. Second, Jesus' teaching in this chapter presents his death and resurrection as the focal point of all Scripture, inviting us to see the whole Bible through the lens of his saving work. Third, Jesus' resurrection prepares for the spread of the gospel "to all nations" (Luke 24:47) and thus sets the stage for Luke's second volume, Acts. Finally, the closing verses of this chapter remind us of the only right response to the truth that Jesus is risen: joy-filled worship of the God who has sent his Son to be our Savior!

The Big Picture

Luke 24 calls us to joyful faith in Jesus by affirming the historical reality and theological significance of his resurrection.

Reflection and Discussion

Read through the complete passage for this study, Luke 24. Then review the questions below and write your notes on them concerning this section of Luke's Gospel. (For further background, see the *ESV Study Bible*, pages 2012–2014, or visit esv.org.)

1. The Earliest Eyewitnesses of Jesus' Resurrection (24:1–12)

What details from these verses indicate that the earliest eyewitnesses did not expect Jesus to be raised from the dead?

What kinds of evidence did these eyewitnesses see and hear that changed their thinking?

2. Jesus Persuades Skeptics on the Emmaus Road (24:13–35)

While some details of this section are puzzling (see Luke 24:16, 28–31), it is clear that the disciples Jesus encounters are filled with grief and confusion. Based on verses 19–24, how would you describe the states of mind and heart they had experienced?

According to Luke 24:25–35, what two kinds of evidence does Jesus provide to help these disciples embrace the reality of his resurrection?

3. Jesus Provides Further Evidence of His Resurrection (24:36–43)

According to Luke 24:34, the people to whom Jesus appears in verse 36 are already convinced that he "has risen indeed." How, then, might we explain their reaction in verses 37–38? (Hint: the first half of verse 41 provides strong clues.)

How does Jesus persuade his followers (1) that he really is alive physically, and not just spiritually, and (2) that he is the same person they knew before?

Some people question the reality of Jesus' resurrection by saying, "Jesus' disciples were naive, prescientific people." Others suggest, "Jesus' disciples were so grief-stricken that they were willing to believe anything." What details from these verses, or from Luke 24 as a whole, argue against such conclusions?

4. Jesus Prepares His People for Faith, Obedience, and Mission (24:44–53)

According to Luke 24:44–53, what kinds of things will we believe when Christ opens our minds to understand the Scriptures? What kinds of things will we do?

The task of worldwide mission Jesus assigns his people in Luke 24:47 is staggering in its scope and importance. According to verses 44–53, what does Jesus do for us or give to us that will sustain us in this task?

Read through the following three sections on *Gospel Glimpses, Whole-Bible Connections*, and *Theological Soundings*. Then take time to consider the *Personal Implications* these sections may have for you.

▶ Gospel Glimpses

THE GREAT REVERSAL. In Luke's first chapter we learn that God is working to bring down "the mighty" and exalt "those of humble estate" (Luke 1:52). Similarly, Jesus teaches that a great reversal, to be confirmed at the final judgment, begins when sinners repent: "For everyone who exalts himself will be humbled, and he who humbles himself will be exalted" (14:11; 18:14). In his crucifixion and resurrection, Jesus has fully experienced this reversal: he has suffered, enduring the humiliation we deserve; and he has entered "into his glory," so that we might share in his exaltation (24:26). When Jesus calls us to lay down our lives in the hope of future glory (9:24–26), he is calling us to pursue a path that he has already walked.

SAVIOR OF THE WORLD. Twice in Luke 24:46 Jesus recalls his crucifixion, saying that it was necessary for him to "suffer" and to "rise from the *dead*." Yet despite these clear reminders of the horrific death he endured just days earlier, Jesus' next thought is not of vengeance. Instead, he longs for the blessings he has won to be extended to sinners everywhere, as "repentance and forgiveness of sins [are] proclaimed in his name to all nations" (v. 47). These words not only summarize the mission of the church but also capture the heart of our Redeemer, who has come "to seek and to save the lost" (19:10). Worldwide redemption is the church's mission—but first, it is the Savior's passion.

▶ Whole-Bible Connections

ONE STORY, ONE PLAN, ONE HERO. In Luke 24, Jesus teaches his disciples that their Bible, our Old Testament, is a unified whole whose parts point to, and find their fulfillment in, him. On the road to Emmaus, he speaks of "things concerning himself" found in "all the Scriptures" (v. 27). Later he links "the Law of Moses and the Prophets and the Psalms"—a reference to the entire Hebrew Old Testament—to his death, resurrection, and saving work (vv. 44–47). Paul similarly indicates that all Scripture is "able to make [us] wise for salvation through faith in Christ Jesus" (2 Tim. 3:15; compare Heb. 1:1–2). From beginning to end, God's Word is intended to increase our dependence on the saving mercy that God alone can provide—mercy that finds its ultimate expression in the work of his Son. The New Testament coalesces with the Old in this, the two Testaments together making one coherent, Christ-centered Bible.

KNOWN IN THE BREAKING OF BREAD. Despite being a guest of the two disciples on the Emmaus road, at mealtime Jesus performs the actions of a host (Luke 24:30), just as he had at the feeding of the 5,000 (9:16) and at the Last Supper (22:19). On each of these occasions, Jesus uses a meal to signify his fellowship[1] with his people, as well as his faithfulness to provide for us what we cannot supply ourselves. This pattern was anticipated in the Old Testament, where the covenant with Israel was confirmed when Moses and the elders "beheld God, and ate and drank" (Ex. 24:11), and where worshipers longed for the blessing of eating in God's presence (Ps. 23:5–6). This longing will be fulfilled at the "marriage supper of the Lamb" (Rev. 19:9), when Jesus will serve us (Luke 12:37) as we "eat and drink at [his] table" (Luke 22:30). Through faith and repentance, we can begin even now to taste his presence and provision: "If anyone hears my voice and opens the door, I will come in to him and eat with him, and he with me" (Rev. 3:20).

> ## Theological Soundings

THE REALITY OF JESUS' RESURRECTION. As is the case with his death, Jesus' resurrection must be a physical and historical reality if it is to have any spiritual significance. Christian teaching therefore rejects suggestions that Jesus' resurrection is a myth, the result of mass hallucination, or an event that is somehow spiritually true even if it did not occur physically. As in our day, Jesus' first followers were reluctant to believe that a dead man could live again (Luke 24:4, 11, 41). In fact, Luke goes out of his way to report the concrete, detailed evidence that persuaded the first eyewitnesses to embrace the truth that "the Lord has risen indeed" (v. 34).

THE ROOTS OF TRINITARIAN DOCTRINE. As Luke 3:22–4:14 introduced the concept of the Trinity, Luke 24:49–53 confirms that Trinitarian thinking was in place from the earliest days of the church. In verse 49, Jesus speaks to his followers of three distinct divine persons: himself ("I am sending"), his "Father," and the Holy Spirit ("*the promise* of my Father;" compare Acts 2:33). Yet Luke 24:52–53 indicates that Jesus and the Father are equally worthy of worship; since biblical teaching abhors the notion of worshiping anyone other than the one true God, this implies a fundamental unity between the Father and the Son. (Though the closing verses of Luke's Gospel do not explicitly say so, the Spirit shares in this unity as well; see Acts 5:3–4, 9.) When the church stated this teaching more systematically in later centuries, it was not inventing new doctrine but expressing truth already present in Scripture.

> ## Personal Implications

Take time to reflect on the implications of Luke 24 for your own life today. Consider what you have learned that might lead you to praise God, repent of sin, and trust more deeply in his gracious promises. Make notes below on the personal implications for your walk with the Lord of the (1) *Gospel Glimpses*, (2) *Whole-Bible Connections*, (3) *Theological Soundings*, and (4) this passage as a whole.

1. Gospel Glimpses

2. Whole-Bible Connections

3. Theological Soundings

4. Luke 24

As You Finish This Unit . . .

Take a moment now to ask for the Lord's blessing and help as you continue in this study of Luke. And take a moment also to look back through this unit of study, to reflect on some key things that the Lord may be teaching you—and perhaps to highlight and underline these things to review again in the future.

Definitions

[1] **Fellowship** – A deep commitment to shared life and love, involving partnership (in shared goals), participation (in one another's joys and sorrows), and connection (often illustrated in Scripture in terms of the relationships among parts of the body or between the head and the body).

Week 12: Summary and Conclusion

▲

As we conclude our study, we will summarize what God teaches us through Luke's Gospel as a whole. Then we will consider several questions that will help us to reflect on various Gospel Glimpses, Whole-Bible Connections, and Theological Soundings that characterize the entire book.

The Big Picture of Luke

Luke's Gospel (like its companion volume, Acts) invites us to be part of the worldwide spread of salvation through Jesus. To strengthen us for the challenges this involves, Luke demonstrates that Jesus brings to fulfillment all of God's saving purposes.

Luke 1:1–9:50 shows us that Jesus is fully prepared for his task, which is not simply to proclaim salvation but to accomplish it. He is the Son of God, more powerful than the greatest of prophets—and yet destined to die. As Jesus' disciples, we will inherit great blessing, but we must also take up a cross of our own.

In 9:51–19:27, Luke provides a narrative of Jesus' journey to Jerusalem, and thus to his death. Along the way, Jesus reorients our vision of God's character and priorities, calling us to reflect this vision in our lives. Through parables (many found only in Luke) and through conflict with opponents, Jesus reveals both the extreme demands and the extravagant grace that characterize life in God's kingdom.

Finally, in Luke 19:28–24:53 we read a detailed account of Jesus' ministry in Jerusalem, culminating in his crucifixion and resurrection. Jesus clearly warns of the tragic consequences of rejecting him, but the overall impact of Luke's narrative is to call people everywhere—including the last, the least, and the lost—to put their trust in Jesus. Thus the Gospel ends on a joyful note, with the promise that Jesus will send the Holy Spirit, who will empower God's people to proclaim "repentance and forgiveness of sins . . . in [Jesus'] name to all nations" (24:47).

Read through the following three sections on *Gospel Glimpses*, *Whole-Bible Connections*, and *Theological Soundings*. Then take time to consider the *Personal Implications* these sections may have for you.

▶ Gospel Glimpses

"My spirit rejoices in God my Savior" (Luke 1:47). For Luke, these words capture the wonder of the gospel. Our sin represents a great debt which we could never repay (7:42; 11:4), but God has sent his Son to rescue us from all its consequences: spiritual, physical, and relational. The grace of this gospel is expressed through paradox: those who humble themselves are exalted (14:11; 18:14), those who see their sin most clearly experience the greatest joy (7:44–50), and Jesus endures the weakness and shame of the cross before he enters his glory (9:22; 24:26).

Has our study of Luke given you a new appreciation for the breadth (God's willingness to redeem people of all kinds) and depth (God's willingness to forgive even the worst of sins) of God's saving grace? How so?

What particular passages or themes in Luke deepened or strengthened your grasp of God's grace to us through Jesus?

From beginning to end, Luke's Gospel makes it clear that "all the Scriptures" (Luke 24:27) are fulfilled in Jesus. His life, death, and resurrection accomplish God's single plan of salvation, by which the redemption of Israel (1:68; 24:21) results in blessing to the nations (2:29–32; 24:47) under a King whose reign will never end (1:33). In short, Jesus is the answer to every promise God has ever made in "the Law of Moses and the Prophets and the Psalms" (24:44).

Many Old Testament promises, prophecies, and patterns of action prepare for, and find fulfillment in, the work of Jesus. Which of these stand out to you at the conclusion of our study? Were any of these connections new to you, or perhaps even surprising?

Which of these connections between Luke's Gospel and the Old Testament has most deeply impacted your understanding of the Bible as a unified whole, revealing a single plan of redemption? Why?

As you look to Jesus in the present for the redemption that he provides, what texts or themes from Luke help you to look forward to an even greater experience of redemption in the future?

▶ **Theological Soundings**

As one of four Spirit-inspired accounts of Jesus' life and ministry, Luke's Gospel makes a rich contribution to Christian theology. Numerous doctrines and themes are developed, clarified, and reinforced throughout Luke, including the nature of Scripture, the deity and humanity of Jesus Christ, justification by grace through faith, and the return of Christ.

Have your theological beliefs shifted in any way, whether major or minor, as a result of studying Luke's Gospel? How so?

What aspects of Jesus' person (who he is) and work (what he accomplishes through his life, death, and resurrection) stand out to you as particularly important in Luke?

How has this study deepened your understanding of the nature and character of (1) God the Father and (2) God the Holy Spirit?

What has Luke's Gospel taught you about the human condition apart from God's grace and therefore about our need of redemption?

Personal Implications

God gave us Luke's Gospel to transform us. How is God using this study to call you to new ways of giving praise to him, turning away from sin, or trusting more firmly in his promises? As you reflect on our study as a whole, what other implications do you see for your life?

Two themes mentioned in Week 1 of our study deserve reflection here: (1) How is God calling you to be part of the worldwide spread of the Christian message? (2) How has Luke's Gospel strengthened you to follow Jesus despite hardship and humiliation?

Look back to the questions already asked in this week's study concerning Gospel Glimpses, Whole-Bible Connections, and Theological Soundings. What implications for life flow from your reflections on these questions?

_____

_____

_____

_____

_____

_____

Based on your study of Luke's Gospel, how would you complete the following statement? "I rejoice to entrust all that I am to Jesus, and to honor him as Lord, because...."

_____

_____

_____

_____

_____

_____

▶ **As You Finish Studying Luke . . .**

We rejoice with you as you complete this study of Luke's Gospel! May what you have learned go with you day by day throughout your life. Now we would greatly encourage you to study the Word of God on a weekly, and even daily, basis. To continue your study of the Bible, we invite you to consider other books in the *Knowing the Bible* series, and to visit www.knowingthebibleseries.org.

Lastly, we encourage you to occasionally take time to look back through this study, reviewing notes that you have written, and reflecting again on the key themes that the Lord has taught you about himself and about his Word. We pray that these things may become a treasure for you now and in days to come—in the name of Jesus, God's chosen Messiah, who has come "to seek and to save the lost" (Luke 19:10). Amen.